LOSE WEIGHT
THINK SLIM

LOSE WEIGHT
THINK SLIM

WITH **PAUL GOLDIN**

Change the way you think about
food to control your weight permanently!

B❋XTREE

First published in Great Britain in 1995 by
Boxtree Ltd, Broadwall House,
21 Broadwall, London SE1 9PL

The right of Paul Goldin to be identified as
Author of this work has been asserted by him in
accordance with the Copyright, Designs and
Patents Act 1988

1 3 5 7 9 10 8 6 4 2

ISBN 0 7522 1672 4

Cover designed by Shoot That Tiger!
Typeset by SX Composing Ltd, Rayleigh, Essex
Printed and bound in Great Britain by
Cox and Wyman Ltd, Reading

A CIP catalogue entry for this book is
available from the British Library

Advice to the reader

Before following any medical, dietary or exercise advice contained in this book, it is recommended that you consult your doctor if you suffer from any health problems or special conditions or are in any doubt.

Contents

Acknowledgements

First and foremost I would like to thank my wife Helen and our daughter Katie Jane, who inspire me every single day of my life – and who also make sure I don't eat too much!

I would also like to thank Richard and John, the developers of Neuro Linguistic Programming – and, of course, Milton H. Erickson, who sadly is no longer with us – all of whom have been the greatest mentors of all my long years studying and practising behavioural psychology.

Then I must acknowledge my huge debt to the thousands of patients who have placed their trust in me and in my methods; their experiences and my work with them has been a never-ending and profoundly satisfying journey of discovery.

Recently, Robert and Joan have come and joined us in our work with our network of Ideal Weight Clubs. Driven by the vast number of people who want to break their obsessive 'diet cycles', this project is growing faster than we could have ever imagined. Thanks also to all our counsellors.

But the last word of thanks must go to my friend Malcolm, whose organisational, interview and writing skills have driven this book forward. A hard task master, he has relentlessly motivated me to share with you, the reader, as many techniques as possible for painlessly and permanently shedding the excess weight within which the Ideal You has always been trapped.

Introduction: Developing the Ideal Weight Programme

This is perhaps the most unusual diet book you will ever come across. It is a diet book with no specific recipes, and no lists of forbidden and unforbidden food. But using the techniques laid out in this book, you will be able to achieve the body shape and size you have always wanted. By following my instructions, you will attain your Ideal Weight.

With this book comes a tape, which contains personal sessions with me to reinforce all you will learn in this book about achieving your Ideal Weight. But first I would like you to read the book, as this will make the tape work so much better. When you are ready, I will give you special instructions as to how to use the tape to reinforce the Ideal Weight Programme as you will have been following it in this book. But for now, read on!

We are born with only three fears – the fear of loud

noises, the fear of falling and the fear of not having enough to eat.

Some of us experience occasional reminders of the first two of these and, for an unfortunate few, they may develop into phobias. But these problems are usually far from central to the lives of even those afflicted.

However, the third inborn fear, that of not having enough food, has grown into an international obsession. It is a scandal of phenomenal proportions that the basic fuel for the body has become a poison for the mind. While so-called "undeveloped" countries have a food fear based on grim reality, the people of the "developed" world are trapped in the ultimate vicious cycle of our age – food, diet and fatness.

You are far, far from alone in your anxieties and difficulties regarding food, diet and fatness.

Say it to yourself now: 'I am far, far from alone in my anxieties and difficulties regarding food, diet and fatness'.

If that seemed odd, or even silly, then that's OK. You don't yet know how I work – and how we are going to be working closely together throughout this book and tape.

You see, the vast majority of people already know the basics of why they are having anxieties and difficulties regarding food, diet and fatness.

The problem is that very few people have the psychological resources to act on this knowledge and do something about their weight problem. Old habits die hard! But by following my Ideal Weight Programme, you will finally discover the way to painless, permanent and health-enhancing weight loss. By focusing on the psychological management of your weight, you will achieve a major break-through in losing weight.

The reasons why you will find my approach unique – and uniquely effective – are several but remarkably simple. Everything we will be doing together will be explained and justified, and there are plenty of examples and exercises to make sure you get the message.

Mind over matter

If you think a primarily psychological approach to weight loss is bunkum and hocus pocus – and you have probably been conditioned this way – then let me give you a challenge: *Stop eating more than your body needs.*

It's as simple as that! If you just stopped eating more than your body needs, then you really would be 'cured' of your weight problems. But telling people what to do and people actually wanting to do some-thing – and going on to achieve it – are very different things.

Even if you are not a smoker you will have seen prominent government health warnings on cigarette advertisements. Most of them clearly state that you are risking a horrible premature death. After a while, however, people hardly notice these negative mes-sages, and smoke on regardless. It's just the same with being told to eat less food.

There are many, many diet systems on offer. In the US alone, at least five or six new diet books are published every month. At my last check, more than 29,800 diet programmes were registered.

However relentlessly packaged and promoted they are, though, the vast majority of these diet programmes do not work. Those who use them end up following the classic 'yo-yo', or 'trampoline' process of dieting: whatever pounds you manage to lose bounce back at you with a vengeance. Many of you will have been through this esteem-sapping process, perhaps many times.

Another term for the cycle is the 'feast or famine' experience, which our ancestors knew in ancient times when food resources often varied between plenty and poverty. Essentially, the body will reluctantly lose a few pounds if starved and then eagerly pile them back on – and more – when the strict regime is relaxed.

In fact, the feast or famine cycle is one of the key – and false – foundations of diet thinking to date. The dieter first starves him or herself and then binges when the body can't take any more. Simply put, he or she has lost control of normal healthy eating.

This book, although geared towards painless and permanent weight loss, has to touch on a great many other things. You need to take – or regain – control of your life. Controlling your weight by learning to do this will come about by understanding the connection between mind and body. Controlling your weight will be just one of the lasting benefits for you.

You will come to recognize the difference between the workings of the conscious and subconscious mind. The conscious mind is simply a term we use to describe specifically what you are thinking and doing at a given moment. The subconscious mind is every-thing else – and it is infinitely larger. It has no conception of time.

Do not worry if this seems a little irrelevant or heavy going. As you read on and learn to use your tape, everything will begin to fall into place.

The most important thing for now is to realize that you have not failed in your efforts so far to control your weight permanently. You are not alone in your experience; the systems have failed you – and so many like you. That you are now on the Ideal Weight Programme is proof that you are not a failure. You are trying and very soon you will feel and see the results, for by coming this far you are already well into the early stages of a journey with real and happy destina-tions of your own choosing.

You are already beyond the reaches of the yo-yo-ing 'Get Fat' weight loss organizations, and under-stand some of the awful flaws in the 'Get Fat' diet programme books.

Let me illustrate why so many other diets fail with real life experiences from my clinic.

Sometimes thin people contact me and ask me to help them gain weight. I have sent several of them along to various weight loss organizations. At first they have painfully dropped a few pounds, only to see the weight, plus some extra, rapidly come back on once the artificial regime has ceased. By repeating the process, they have yo-yo-ed their way to their desired heavier selves!

You are a member of the Late 20th Century De-veloped Country Cult of Food, Diet and Fatness. Together we are going to work to deprogramme you from that.

The rubbish that we swallow

If you live in the UK, Ireland, or the US – the places where I have lived the longest – then it is quite likely that you swallow an average of 100lbs of fat and 100lbs of sugar per year.

But this is not going to be a recipe book. Just as food manufacturers bulk out their wares with fat and sugar – and with many other useless or dangerous substances – so many diet books pad out their pages with recipes. It's easier to do that than offer their readers anything really new!

But as well as the useless foods and the lists of un-appetizing menus, the worst rubbish that the diet industry asks us to swallow are some of its central myths.

Through the Ideal Weight Programme you will realize that orthodox dieting makes you fat. I believe that weighing scales are for cattle and sheep. People who diet and measure their progress by weighing themselves all the time put on weight! They look at the scales and see that they have lost a few pounds, then rush out and binge on food to celebrate! Of course, those pounds come right back. Or else, if they haven't managed to lose the weight they wanted to lose, they feel guilty and go off and eat to console themselves.

Diet advice that fails to alter an individual's food belief systems is just meaningless.

'Oh, so what he is going to do is insult everyone else's weight loss system and say that only his one works,' is what you may be thinking by this stage.

That would not be quite right. I will be pointing out a lot of the nonsense that masquerades as health

14

advice; however, the vast majority of the diet detail of which I approve is already readily available elsewhere. That I freely acknowledge, and I am not going to repeat it here.

Where the key problem has always lain is in enabling people, happily and permanently, to integrate good dietary advice and sound eating patterns into their lifestyles.

What gives me the right to be 'teaching' you?

I've never been substantially overweight. So, unlike all the born-again thinnies with their latest diet and exercise programmes, I can't preach the gospel of my own miraculous waistline reawakening.

I haven't got a doctorate in nutrition and neither am I a brilliant cook. In fact, the food that I eat is no big deal to me; eating is mainly just something I do to get along, even though I enjoy what I eat – as will you.

What I do claim to be is a communicator. I have practised behavioural psychology for more than forty years. My father was a psychiatrist, and we moved from France to Britain as war loomed.

I went to study medicine at the University of London and in 1952 obtained my first degree, in Psychology and Logic. By this time the functions and power of the human mind had become my main interest.

During this period I began to present lecture demonstrations to fellow students entitled 'Powerful Strategies with Predictable Outcomes'. This was the first version of a lecture, developed into 'The Amazing World of Paul Goldin', which has run in theatres across the world ever since, often to audiences of 10,000 and more.

But it is from my continual work with private patients that my knowledge and stimulation has come. And the more time I spend with people one-to-one, the more I see that the waste of human potential through poor communication is colossal.

Some of the most demanding work I have undertaken is in the area of operant conditioning, a subject better known as brainwashing.

During a time spent researching and lecturing at the University of Hawaii in the 1970s, my colleagues and I were increasingly being drawn into 'de-programming', or 'exit counselling' work.

Our task was to reintegrate cult members into mainstream society. It was an era when such dubious organizations were growing at a frightening rate and our role was to put people back together again.

Although sometimes very heavy going, these challenges gave us fantastic insights into the structure of human belief systems – and the best methods for changing or modifying them.

The single greatest of the challenges came in 1978 when a team of us was sent into the South American jungle in the aftermath of the horrendous Jonestown massacre, when many hundreds of the followers of the cult leader Jim Jones obeyed his command to commit mass suicide by drinking cyanide. Our task was to work with the severely disturbed survivors, the living who had refused.

As well as a time for massive growth in cult

16

activity, another industry was experiencing huge expansion during the 1970s, particularly in the US. This was the diet and fitness industry. Vanity was leading to insanity, particularly from the viewpoint of us psychologists who were dealing with eating disorders and overweight anxieties as part of our everyday workload.

It was then that I made the mental connection that was to lead to the development and refinement of the Ideal Weight Programme as it exists and helps people today.

I never worked with a fat Moonie, nor an overweight Hari Krishna, nor a Scientologist who crept downstairs in the middle of the night to raid the fridge. Whatever the weirdness of the beliefs drummed into them, hang-ups about food were not among them.

Conventional society, with all its conflicting and distorted food messages, had been left behind. Most people would argue that turning your back on family and friends to stand, shave headed, on a street corner selling pencils is not the best step a person can take.

But for them, food was simply no longer an issue. There was no anxiety surrounding nutrition. Food was simply something not consciously thought about – a fuel to be put into the mouth to keep the body going and nothing else.

Why shouldn't this be the same for all of us? I set to work developing a programme to relieve people of the stress surrounding food, helping them both to achieve their full potential and to enable them to enjoy what they eat more than they ever did before!

1

How does the Ideal Weight Programme work?

Let me start with a favourite parable of mine.

Once upon a time there was a little bunny rabbit who came out of his burrow to find himself stuck in a briar patch. He could see the beautiful open meadows and the gently rolling hills beyond and he longed to play with the other little rabbits he could see frolicking on the open grasslands beyond. But he was stuck in a briar patch.

At nights he used to dream of the fun he should be having but, every morning, he had to back off as the thorns pricked into his sides and hurt. The briars were a barrier that were keeping him away from the wonderful world that he could see he should be enjoying . . .

There is a briar patch in many people's lives. For some it might be fear. For others it might be in the areas of health or relationships.

My job as a psychologist has always been to guide people through their own briar patch. That is all there is to it. There is nothing sinister or demanding involved – or, absolutely crucially, nothing that you do not already want to do, even if you feel you have failed to do it many times in the past.

There is no sense of deprivation with the Ideal Weight Programme. In fact, you are being freed at last from the oppressive Cult of Food, Diet and Fatness.

It is important that you approach our work together with an open and receptive mind. With those preconditions you are much more likely to succeed.

Do not struggle and concern yourself unnecessarily with the order in which the course is presented. It is a therapeutic process that we are putting together, not the preparation for an exam. You will work at your own pace and be taking it one day at a time. It will work if you follow it properly, and every point is repeatedly reinforced.

You will notice there is a degree of repetition. This is deliberate. Repetition is the mother of skill.

There are also plenty of things for you to do. Please do them. They are not included just to fill up space, like the fat and the sugar in junk food, nor the endless recipes in diet books. I have written this book for a reason – if just selling people tapes by mail order was the way forward, then I would be lying with a tape recorder on a beach in Barbados, not sitting huddled over my keyboard during a typical Irish winter!

Remember that the Ideal Weight Programme is the

culmination of more than forty years' work of helping people with their problems. It has been presented in seminar format to combined audiences of more than 3,000 and thousands more are now attending Ideal Weight Clubs every week. Many more people have seen my Lose Weight Think Slim video.

For some of you this book and tape will form a self-contained home study programme – you and I working together to overcome your overweight difficulty painlessly and permanently. For others it will act as a support and top-up mechanism to what you may learn at a seminar or club, or watching my video. Both are absolutely fine and will work for you.

Remember most of all that this, unlike the rocky road of dieting you have been on up until now, is a new journey into endless freedom.

Every journey begins with the first step

In each chapter of this book, I will help you to understand more about how you have the power to achieve your Ideal Weight. At the end of each chapter, you will find a few simple mental exercises to reinforce what you will be learning, and prepare you for using the tape.

We are going to start work together right now. You will need a pen and paper. You will also need about thirty minutes. Please do not continue unless you have this time. If you do not, then put the book to one side and come back later when at least thirty minutes is available. Otherwise, please fetch a pen and paper before you read on.

The Affirmations

We shall be using and re-using these positive statements about yourself. They will gradually become part of you and they will become automatic. At this stage they will seem awkward and alien. Let me illustrate this as we begin.

Take your pen in the hand with which you do NOT usually write and at the top of your page write your name. It will probably be rather difficult, but just about legible.

Next to it write your name with the hand with which you usually write. Compare the two. If you were to lose your habitual writing hand, or if it were to become paralyzed, you would be able to reproduce the superior writing with your other hand within a surprisingly short period. Necessity is the mother of invention; repetition is the mother of skill.

Now, with whatever degree of uncertainty – or even slight embarrassment – that you may feel, please copy out the following ten affirmations on to your sheet of paper:

1. *I can easily lose weight.*

2. *I can easily lose weight simply by the changing of my eating habits and these will become permanent.*

3. *From now on I will incorporate a very simple activity programme into my life, be it walking, swimming, or whatever.*

4. *Because I like myself, from now on I will choose healthy and nutritious food.*

5. *I am responsible for me. I am responsible for my body and I am responsible for the food that I eat.*

6. *From now on, I will be able to control and express my emotions.*

7. *From now on, I will start to achieve and maintain a healthy shape, size and figure – the shape and size I would like to be.*

8. *I am learning to love myself because I fully understand that unless I love myself, I cannot love others.*

9. *From this day onwards I shall become a successful individual. I can achieve my goals. As I think, so I shall become.*

10. *I am becoming aware of myself. I have developed control.*

Thank you for doing that. We are now really working together. But before we move on, there is some more thinking and writing I would like you to do:

1. *Before today is out (first thing tomorrow if this is late at night), write down something you have been delaying for some time now – and do it. It could be making an awkward phone call to someone you owe an apology. It could be tidying up the mess in the cupboard under the*

stairs. Pick something that is genuinely preying on your mind – and get it done, today.

2. *Imagine* . . . Visualize the shape and size you will be if you don't follow through with the reprogramming exercises.

3. Write down five good reasons why you MUST lose weight. Go back over them several times.

4. Write down your own answer to this question: 'What is the most important thing to me in my life?'

5. Write down what you understand by the following statement: 'The past does not equal tomorrow'.

7. Close your eyes and, first, imagine what you would be like in five years if you continue to gain weight as you have been in the past. Now, change this picture. Visualize the size and shape you would like to be within just a few months.

7. Step forward into the future . . . see yourself slimmer and happier.

Thank you again. It is very likely that you found all that rather difficult and still remain unsure. But just remember what you used to do at school, or when you were last studying. You used to be asked to think carefully about all manner of things and to write them down as an aid to visualizing, learning and remembering. It is likely that you were asked to do this about all manner of things, except the most important task that faces children and young people – looking after themselves and making the best of themselves. You see, we are not doing anything artificial or odd here. We are merely filling a huge omission in most people's upbringings.

Let me summarize this first section of exercises together with an example. It is as if we are learning to swim and this was just the first clumsy splash in the shallow end. As the programme unfolds, you will become a very proficient swimmer indeed.

2

Calories in, calories out: why we become fat

We become fat because we eat too much. By putting too much food into our mouths, we ingest more energy (calories) than we can expend. But remember the equation: calories in, calories out! You will get fat if you take in more food than your body can use.

These things are obvious, but people have for years been trying to distance themselves from the truth. 'Oh but it's my metabolism,' they say. If you accept the notion of a metabolism – picture a boiler that burns energy in the form of fuel – then you must accept that the boiler needs just a certain amount of energy. What is left over becomes fat. Simply put, you are fat, therefore, because you eat too much food for that boiler to use up!

'I'm overweight because I'm a businessman,' says the corpulent executive in the bulging pin-stripe suit.

He may be fat because he stuffs himself at the hotel breakfasi bar, at the restaurant power lunch and at the evening trade mission reception. But he is fat because he eats too much, not because he is a successful businessman. Many of his colleagues – and his business rivals – still manage to be slim.

'I'm fat because I've got four children and a husband to look after. All I've got time for is picking at snacks,' says the genuinely busy and harassed housewife. But she is fat because she snacks on a lot of high-calorie junk food.

'I'm fat because I simply haven't got the time any more to exercise,' says the busy ex-sportsperson, relaxing among friends with a glass of beer in hand.

But it isn't the lack of exercise that makes the ex-sportsperson fat. Have you seen the gigantic Japanese sumo wrestlers on television? They are the rare example of sportspeople – indeed, any people – who deliberately choose to be extremely overweight. Their titanic bulk is believed to help their struggles in the wrestling ring and, while they take a great deal of exercise, they stuff themselves with high calorie stew and beer. Sportspeople are just like everyone else. They get fat when they eat too much!

Perhaps you will have made up your own excuse by now – I am not going to try to exhaust every single possibility. People, are very ingenious when it comes to explaining why they are overweight. But I want you to be honest and say now: 'I am overweight because I eat too much for my body's needs.'

You will not love me for having forced that issue. It will probably have caused a degree of resentment – and maybe even guilt.

Of course there will be an element of pressure, re-sentment, or guilt about how you feel with regard to food. You need to accept that this is the case.

A large part of this book is about what encourages, suggests, pesters and, ultimately, forces people to eat too much for their bodies' needs. Understand these processes and you are on the way to conquering the guilt. Release the guilt and you are starting to release the anxiety about food, diet and fatness. Overcome the anxiety and you are releasing the urges, the binges and the process that keep you wrapped in a bandage of fat.

If you cut a finger, you wrap it in a bandage. If your emotions are wounded, you can wrap them in a ban-dage of fat. But I want to show you a way out of this. You may have heard the expression, 'Stop the bleed-ing to start the healing'. Let's look at some of the things that inflict those wounds.

Food as culture: the hard sell

By 'culture', I am not asking you to visualize images of expensive paintings, great works of literature and stately academic figures in ivory towers or corridors of power.

I am talking about the social influences over the way we behave. Both the process and the results can be nasty and harmful, as well as productive.

Let's look at how this connects to food. During the late 1950s, I was called in by a major US cinema chain to observe and advise on a new form of advertising that was under development.

The theory was to 'pump' visual images into the subconscious mind faster than the conscious mind would register. The new technique involved cutting extra frames into the existing film and repeating the same, or a set, of extra images at regular intervals.

The first experiment I observed placed the picture of a well-known brand of soft drink at regular intervals within the regular feature film. No member of the audience later commented on noticing anything unusual, and there were no complaints.

During the first half of the film, the cinema heating was turned up. At the interval, the usual range of soft drinks was available at the refreshment bar, with the selected brand being given no special prominence.

NONE OF THE OTHER BRANDS WAS DRUNK. Much higher than usual overall sales were recorded, with all of them being for the selected brand. This drink is a sticky, sugar-laden substance with absolutely no recognized food value whatsoever. It is world famous and advertising people talk of its marketing 'success' in terms of reverence and awe.

A little while later, the experiment was repeated but this time with images of popcorn being interspersed with the feature film. During the interval, an entire evening's supply of popcorn sold out within just a few minutes.

This kind of advertising is called subliminal advertising. It is now illegal in most countries. The argument goes that it does not give the consumer a fair chance of making an unforced choice.

I happen to believe that this was a correct decision by the authorities – but it is a very thin line indeed and one that is, in effect, crossed every day by the cumulative nature of the barrage of advertising images we receive.

It is vital that you understand the power of subliminal advertising. It gives you an immediate access to and an understanding of the power of the subconscious mind. You should need no other proof – although plenty of other examples will be presented to you during the course of the Ideal Weight Programme.

As to the thin line between 'legal' and 'illegal' advertising, let me describe for you another classic case from the history of brand development and brand awareness.

If you are watching a blockbuster movie, or a tense football final, on television, the action might suddenly move from the main event to the commercial break. Number one item during that break might be a household name breakfast cereal. It is highly likely that the next time you are buying cereal, that brand will catch your eye.

Advertising like this is hypnosis being used as the backbone of a brainwashing campaign. The number one advertising spots in breaks during prime time events on television are extremely expensive because of the enormity of the captive audience. You see, there is a very thin line between advertising which is held to be culturally acceptable and advertising which is deemed to be unacceptable.

The huge plus side of all of this is one inescapable fact that was taught and re-taught to me during all my years of 'de-programming' work. It is that whatever methods have been used to enslave can also be used to empower. In other words, what the mind can do, the mind can undo.

Let me give you one more example of my observations and work from within the commercial world of food and drink retailing. During the 1980s, again in the US, I was consulted by one of the leading supermarket chains to see whether I could do anything to lower the rate of 'shrinkage' – an industry term, better known to you and me as plain old shoplifting.

So I took their piped-in music and interlaced it with messages such as 'don't steal – you will get caught and sent to prison' and 'your children will hate you if you get caught as a shoplifter'.

Just as dogs can pick up sounds inaudible consciously to the human ear, so people's subconscious can pick up messages that they cannot 'hear' as such. Nonsense? Well, the rates of shoplifting immediately dropped by 40 percent!

If anyone out there is still sitting back smugly and thinking 'that's OK, I'm advertising proof, I'm too smart to fall for those kind of tricks', then just read on . . .

'Traditional and wholesome foods' – just how good for you are they?

'Traditional', 'family', 'grandma's', 'mother's', 'farmhouse', 'country', 'old time', 'cottage' . . . images of robust and red-cheeked Victorian farmers, smiling children of yesteryear, grandparental figures all spring to mind. A lovely cosiness of solid values that is still used to sell foods off the supermarket shelves.

But these are also foods that are full of salt and sugar, chemical dyes and preservatives; cheap fats that clog your arteries. They contain sawdust-like grain residues – all that is left after the useful nutrients have been extracted for profitable animal feeds – and meat products from animals pumped full of hormones and drugs.

Why do we eat this stuff? Well, it's traditional, isn't it? This is one of the greatest myths and brainwashing feats of the food industry. And the real tradition of food can be pretty awful too!

Availability, not advertising, has been the key issue regarding food for the vast majority of the world's population since time began. Availability is still the major factor for most people. The majority has to make do with what it gets, while a minority can afford, relatively speaking, to feast. This has been the same for centuries. It has always been only the relatively rich who could feast off the unadulterated produce of the land.

The 'golden age' of traditional and wholesome food for the masses that the marketing men constantly harp back to simply did not exist.

Until a few generations ago, the diet of the vast majority of the Irish consisted chiefly of potatoes. Just across the sea, the majority of the British had bread to supplement their potatoes and maybe a little fatty meat – but still hardly a nourishing diet.

Remember, as we go through these horror stories, that one of the objects of the Ideal Weight Programme is that food should be enjoyable and does have an important social role in our lives.

You may have heard the old expression 'don't shoot the messenger'. What we are doing is confronting some of the misplaced notions that begin

brainwashing us from b… … …
choices about foodstuffs.

Myths that underpin the food…

Before rampant commercialism took o… …
some very good intentions underpinning … …
try recommendations, even though today … seem
rather dubious and have been hijacked by the major
food sellers and manufacturers.

During the early and middle parts of the 20th
century, nutritional deficiency diseases, such as rick-
ets, gradually ceased to be endemic and are now rare
in Britain, Ireland, the US and other Western societies.

What emerged during this era was the concept of
the 'normal', or 'balanced' diet. Some of the scientific
notions behind these concepts have later been shown
to be flawed but the main drive, vital for improved
public health, was simply to get more calories, protein, vitamins and minerals into the stomachs of the
malnourished.

Getting something approximating a fulfilling diet
into children whose ribs had previously been sticking
out was a very good idea indeed.

However, it has left us with a range of myths which
underpin the giant and vested food interests of
today.

To take just four of the main ones (we shall be
catching up on some of the best of the recent and independent food thinking later on): until very recently
meat, particularly red meat, was always thought of as

...cent great idea – hugely nourishing and a ...perb source of protein and minerals. But the kind and amount of fat found in this meat is a major contributor to heart disease. The same goes for many kinds of cheese.

As for milk, the mass consumption of large quantities of cow's milk is a relatively recent phenomenon. Cow's milk is to beef up baby cows and, with the huge amounts of fat it contains, it does a very good job, too.

The fourth example is sugar. It is a truly terrible food. The best the hard-sell merchants have been able to come up with is that it gives you energy. But it also rots your teeth, disrupts your blood sugar levels and, being completely free of any other food value, wastes valuable extra 'calorie space' for something useful. I recently saw a series of advertisements associating sugar with sexy young men. God help us! I hope my wife doesn't abandon me for a bag of sugar!

But there will be no specific recipes or even prohibitions within the Ideal Weight Programme. You will always make up your own mind. A little sugar, occasionally and in moderation, need not be bad for you. But what is more important is the automatic control of your intake of such foods that you are already learning.

The Affirmations

Now that you are beginning to see a little of what we are up against, it is time to tackle our affirmations again. I hope you feel that we are building up your awareness of what is controlling your weight and that you are getting the message that you are in control. We are up against a lot of competition for your eating habits but there is no need for a siege mentality – you have ample resources to attain and maintain your Ideal Weight without struggle, stress, or anxiety.

So, let's pick up that pen and paper again and go through the affirmations. Be strong but relaxed. Feel, hear and see the power of what you are writing. Visualize the new you that you are creating and feel the excitement of the changes that you are beginning to make. Copy them out now:

1. *I can easily lose weight.*

2. *I can easily lose weight simply by changing my eating habits and these will become permanent.*

3. *From now on I will incorporate a very simple activity programme into my life, be it walking, swimming, or whatever.*

4. *Because I love myself, from now on I will choose healthy and nutritious food.*

5. *I am responsible for me. I am responsible for my body and I am responsible for the food that I eat.*

6. *From now on, I will be able to control and express my emotions.*

7. *From now on, I will start to achieve and maintain a healthy shape, size and figure – the shape and size I would like to be.*

8. *I am learning to love myself because I fully understand that unless I love myself I cannot love others.*

9. *From this day onwards I shall become a successful individual. I can achieve my goals. As I think, so I shall become.*

10. *I am becoming aware of myself. I am developing control.*

EFFECTIVE GOAL SETTING
Now, in the last set of exercises, I asked you to write down five good reasons why you must lose weight. Either look at them, if you have saved them, or try to remember what you wrote.

Were they mainly negative or positive reasons? They may have included notions like 'so that I don't strain my heart and die', or 'so that people will stop laughing at me behind my back', or 'so that people will stop thinking I'm useless'.

We will be doing a great deal of work together on

effective goal setting. Learning to set goals is one of the most important ways of getting to where you want to be. The subconscious mind is like an arrow. It shoots straight for its target. So the important thing is to know what your goals are and then to 'set' them clearly in your mind. We are already developing these techniques and will continue to do so.

Another very important aspect, however, is to develop positive goals. Negative motivations are very strong. We are all full of reasons why not to do things. Negative goals cling around each other, just like fat children tend to hang around with each other in the playground.

We are going to do that initial exercise again now. We need five GOOD reasons – that word was there first time round, you just didn't notice it – why you must lose weight.

One or two is not sufficient, and they must be directly positive. Here is an example: 'I can remember when we used to have great fun on holiday playing beach football with the kids. This year I'm, going to have great fun just like that again'.

Do it. You do not have to be in the groups who see arsonists on every street corner or every potential situation being the biggest personal or professional humiliation of your life. You do not have to suffer to grow.

Finally in this exercise section, before we return to the reasons why people become fat, we are going to learn a simple little technique that will put you directly in touch with your body, your hunger and your appetite. Read this through carefully and then try it out a few times.

HOW TO BECOME FRIENDS WITH YOUR TUMMY
Sit down, close your eyes and gently rest a soft, open fist on your tummy. That is about the natural size of your stomach. Feel your stomach being about the size of your fist and feel it that size within you.

Now, stretch your fingers out, feeling the tension build up and press down a little on your tummy. That is the kind of pressure that you build up on your stomach when you gorge yourself, when you eat far more than your body needs. You can feel your stomach stretching and see it, distended and swollen like a balloon. No wonder it hurts sometimes.

Now, relax your hand. Ease off the pressure. Feel and see your stomach shrink as your hand gradually pulls back into a soft, open fist, just resting on your tummy. The pain of all that stretching has gone.

Do this regularly over the next few days. Become friends with your stomach and stop abusing it. Next time you feel the urge to gorge yourself, rather than wait just a little longer until your next balanced meal, just place your soft, open fist on your stomach. You are being kind to your long-overworked stomach and it will be grateful.

Are you a Compulsive Eater? Relax!

Write down your worried thoughts and then write down any sort of positive suggestions which could change them.

(Do this on a weekly basis)

1. Worried thought_____

2. Worried thought_____

3. Worried thought_____

4. Worried thought_____

5. Worried thought_____

6. Worried thought_____

7. Worried thought_____

8. Worried thought_____

9. Worried thought_____

10. Worried thought_____

By acting on these positive suggestions, you will start to stop using food as the answer to your worries.

3
What do we associate with food?

You will now be beginning to understand clearly that not only are you far from alone in being overweight but that there are also clear and specific reasons why this is the case.

But there is a lot more that we must understand before we can really shake off our cloaks of fat once and for all. 'Big is beautiful' is not just a recently dreamed-up slogan of oppressed fatties fighting back. It is also very much part of our culture.

Just this morning I read an article in a newspaper which began 'Tongans are being encouraged to break with a long tradition that big is beautiful. Alarmed by the results of a recent survey showing increasing obesity among the 105,000 people of the South Pacific kingdom, officials have launched a weight-awareness campaign.'

As the people of Tonga have been exposed to feast or famine conditions for numerous generations, they have traditionally associated size with good survival prospects – and hence with attractiveness.

Now, however, with the declining levels of physical activity, the general rise in prosperity and the increasing consumption of sweet and fatty imported foods, the rapid increase in general obesity has been identified as a major cause of diabetes and hypertension – and the problems are reaching epidemic proportions.

We are exporting our Western food culture, our Western rubbish and our Western diseases. What is happening in Tonga today has already happened in many other countries.

Let me ask you to do a spot of quick visualization. Without bringing any particular person to mind – just a strong image of a typical character – please draw yourself a mental picture of an enormously rich international business tycoon.

It is very likely that your imaginary character was of enormous girth. Why is that? Because fat can still be associated with plenty. 'Plenty' used to just mean lots to eat. It now has the more general meaning of wealth itself.

So, you will see that it is not just the present that is encouraging us to be overweight. The widespread poverty and survival demands of our past is doing a pretty good job at keeping the pounds piled on as well.

How you can take control

There is something else that will start to be obvious to you. Stop now for a moment and think about all the diet regimes you have tried over the years. You were a prisoner to them. Just as you have been until now a prisoner of the food culture of your past and your present.

Mr Nasty Diet, Mr Complicated Menu, Mr Grapefruit, Mr Very Expensive and Sickly Milk Shake – they have all been your own cult leaders. You have been going from one state of being out of control of your own life straight into a secondary state of being out of control of your own destiny.

The Ideal Weight Programme is not about taking control away from you. It *is* about *giving* control to you. It does this by giving you choice – the choice to take it or leave it. Until now you have been trapped by the anxiety of not eating. You couldn't walk past a free doughnut stand in a supermarket without having one. Soon you will walk past having full control over your actions, a complete freedom of choice, without teeth clenching and great acts of willpower.

This sense of freedom is very different from how the vast majority of people feel. Most people feel under enormous pressure to conform to a particular shape. A recent study in the US revealed that 70 percent of women felt stressed, depressed and guilty when shown photographs of Naomi Campbell, Kate Moss and other supermodels. These women actually have unusual shapes, though!

In fact, in the time of the old master painters Reubens and Rembrandt, they would have been regarded as freaks. The 'ideal' women of those days were, in our terms, considerably overweight. Don't be caught in the trap of thinking a supermodel's super-thinness is your Ideal Weight!

Men are under attack as well

Men are increasingly far from immune from fads, fashions and utter nonsense. Big muscles and sculpted torsos are in. Arnold, Sly, Van Damme and the pumped-up band who have followed in their wake have seen to that. Men are under artificial shape pressure as never before – and I meet the sufferers in my clinic and at my seminars and clubs.

In a way, men are sometimes under even more severe pressure than women. If they are overweight they do not know which way to turn. Should they be dieting to lose weight, or dieting and pumping iron to gain muscle? Surely all those fantastic powders and pills in the chemists and sportshops will be the answer to all their problems?

Rippling abdominals do not come out of bottles and cartons. They come from genetic disposition and a fantastic volume of sheer hard work. The vast majority of the 'muscle build' products are simply a fantastically exorbitant mixture of chemically flavoured milk powder, sugar and, sometimes, eggs. It is an example of the diet industry expanding into new, crazy and confusing areas.

Food is about everything but eating

So, food as body shape is all the rage. But there are many, many more examples of how food is everything to all people – except a simple fuel mechanism to keep our bodies functioning.

There is food as an introduction – 'Come on in.

Have a cup of tea. Have some biscuits with it. I've got a lovely cake; I'll get some for you.' Before you've even said hello you have been force-fed 30 percent of your daily calorie requirement in unsolicited junk!

Sharing food is a valuable and sociable activity. The family table may be the only focus of family conversation. During times of food scarcity the sharing of food was a great sign of charity and friendship. But forcing refined sugar on our friends is a perversion of these fine traditions. Food as an introduction is just one way that friends can make you fat.

Another is food as courtship. Remember some of your first dates? Did you have a few drinks? Go out for a meal? Did you cook a special meal? Do you associate special times with a special person with eating and drinking?

Then there is food as celebration. Christmas. Birthdays. Special achievements. It's that day again, or didn't we do well – let's go and eat as much as we possibly can!

Now, again, all these associations have very good behavioural and historical explanations. You see it in the animal kingdom – a male bird offers a female bird a dead mouse as the ultimate chat-up line! She falls head over talons in love with him because he has proved he is a good hunter and will provide for their offspring.

And you have heard the expression 'to kill the fatted calf'. It used to mean just that. Special occasions deserved the slaughter and festive preparation of a precious beast, be it a hen, a pig, a calf or a sheep. People had special foods on special occasions. It was a blessed relief from the monotony of their limited diets and the delight of the special food underlined and became deeply associated with their delight at the occasion itself.

These are some ways that food has become associated with pleasure. But there is a danger now that for many people every day is seen as a feast day. It is a big mistake to think that if you are feeling unhappy you can start eating and get some of that Christmas cheer back. This is a perversion of the tradition of food as genuine celebration.

The Affirmations

KEYS TO THE MOST IMPORTANT CHANGES YOU WILL EVER MAKE

By now we are really beginning to get to grips with this overweight issue, aren't we? Have you heard the expression 'a problem shared is a problem solved'? It's not totally true because there is still plenty of work to be done, but it is a great deal easier to solve because the anxiety is fading away and we are working out a thorough plan for permanent success. Have you realized that we are now so far into this planning process that the Ideal Weight Programme is now a very real part of your own life? You will feel this as we go through the affirmations this time. After each one we are going to use them in an even stronger way than before as we explore your own personal strategy, in relation to all the cultural pressure to eat that we have just discussed.

When we have finished this set of affirmations – and there is absolutely no rush – I am going to give you a very powerful tool. Do the affirmations first and I promise you that this tool will make a very real difference to your life when you learn to use it effectively.

Copy out the affirmations as usual on a sheet of paper and involve yourself in the supplementary exercises – this is the start of you developing your own control over what you eat. It is the end of being dictated to. Copy out the affirmation that you already know and then involve yourself with the supplementary exercise.

1. *I can easily lose weight.*

Read this paragraph carefully and then close your eyes and do as I ask. Make a strong mental picture of yourself exactly as you are today. A picture of yourself sitting where you are right now, dressed as you are. Now open your eyes. Close them again and make exactly the same picture. You are sitting in the same place, wearing the same clothes. Have you got that? Good. Now do all of this. Hold the pictures for a little while.

Did that go OK for you? Could you see yourself clearly on both occasions? Were you exactly the same in both? Were you feeling exactly the same? Good.

The thing is, though, that you missed two things. There were two differences that I forgot to tell you about. The first is that the second picture was meant to be exactly a week from now. It will not matter at all but we had better correct my mistake. Close your eyes. Make exactly the same image of yourself. Feel exactly the same. It is a week later, that's all.

That was not difficult at all. Oh . . . but I have still forgotten to tell you about the second difference. My apologies. I forgot because it was very insignificant indeed and you probably didn't notice either.

In the second picture you were one pound lighter than in the first picture. Nobody noticed. There was no effort or trouble on your part and I even forgot to tell you. It just didn't seem important.

That is how difficult the Ideal Weight Programme is. One pound a week, so that no one, least of all yourself, even bothers to think about. 52lbs in a year, if you wish – no effort or thought.

So let's confirm that point once more by writing out:

I can easily lose weight.

2. *I can easily lose weight simply by the changing of my eating habits and these will become permanent.*

The Ideal Weight Programme advocates three balanced meals per day. Think about this for a minute. A balanced breakfast. A balanced lunch and a balanced dinner. It doesn't really deserve more than a moment or two of thought because that's it. So let's just also confirm that:

I can easily lose weight simply by the changing of my eating habits and these will become permanent.

3. *From now I will incorporate a very simple activity programme into my life, be it walking, swimming, cycling or whatever.*

We will be outlining the Ideal Weight Programme's concept of an activity programme later on but if you think that we are going to be turning you into reluctant athletes, then forget it.

We are not talking about strenuous charging about or great big muscles – but you will end up feeling delightfully fit and toned. So feel delightfully fit and toned as we confirm that:

From now I will incorporate a very simple activity programme, be it walking, swimming, or whatever.

4. *Because I love myself, from now on I will choose healthy and nutritious food.*

This might not strike you, on the face of it, as quite as straightforward – but it is, believe me, and by freeing yourself already of that colossal mass of cultural debris, you are already well on the way. There is a lot more support and help to come.

In terms of putting good things automatically into your mouth, just imagine this. You have swum for miles in a very salty sea under a blazing hot sun. You are absolutely parched when you come ashore. Close your eyes now and imagine that thirst and your salt-cracked lips.

You might fancy a glass of water. You might instead have some fizzy pop, a cola drink or a glass of lemonade . . . no more or no less than some liquid chemicals and sugar. All foods and drinks that are pumped up with loads of sugar are of no food value to us. Do you remember those hundreds of brain-washed people who killed themselves for the cult leader Jim Jones by drinking cyanide? They no longer loved themselves and they died in agony. The cyanide was mixed up in lemonade.

So, now that these points are clearer, let's confirm that:

Because I love myself, from now on I will choose healthy and nutritious food.

5. *I am responsible for me. I am responsible for my body and I am responsible for the food that I eat.*

I often run anti-smoking sessions for groups of patients at my clinic. Quite often, at the start of the sessions, when we are having a general discussion about why they want to stop, someone will say something along the lines of 'My Uncle Joe smokes like a chimney and he's still playing golf every day at the age of 85'.

I will pull my handkerchief out of my pocket and go to hand it to the person saying: 'This is a blindfold. Put it on and go outside on to the main road and wander around. You may be lucky and dodge the traffic.'

Having no responsibility with regard to the food that you eat is just as reckless . . . but by coming this far with me I am sure that you have already thrown your blindfold away for good. You can see the road ahead and it is very attractive.

So, with your blindfold well and truly consigned to the dustbin, confirm that:

I am responsible for me. I am responsible for my body and I am responsible for the food that I eat.

6. *From now on I will be able to control and express my emotions.*

We have already developed together one very powerful tool to control your emotions when they threaten to make you binge and gorge.

Let's repeat it right now. Read carefully and then close your eyes and do it. Lay a soft and open fist gently on your tummy. Spread your fingers out. Stretch them and push down. That's the strain you feel when you stretch your stomach to bursting with excess food and drink. See the balloon close to bursting. Feel the pressure. Now relax your hand back into a soft and open fist. Feel the pressure easing. Your stomach feels good. You have stopped abusing it and it likes you again.

At the end of this section there will come another strong tool but first there is still important work to be done on the affirmations. So just confirm that, with all the help you are receiving:

From now on I will be able to control and express my emotions.

7. *From now on, I will start to achieve and maintain a healthy shape, size and figure – the shape and size I would like to be.*

Did you know that your subconscious mind is actually extremely sensible? It is a great deal more sensible than your conscious mind which is struggling to sort out the barrage of events and instincts that are constantly flying past it.

Have you ever heard expressions like 'a woman's instinct', 'my sixth sense told me', 'I had an uneasy feeling', 'something about it told me that . . .'? Or have you ever had an uneasy feeling about something but you went ahead anyway – and it went badly wrong?

There is nothing remotely odd or mysterious about any of these things. They are just a tiny handful of examples about the way that your subconscious guides you. There is one expression that says it better than all others: 'my better instincts told me that . . .'

Now, let's close our eyes again when this paragraph is finished and begin to visualize our own healthy shape, size and figure. Your subconscious is not silly. If you are a woman and you are 5ft 3ins tall with relatively narrow shoulders, it is not going to paint a picture for you of Yasmine Bleeth of 'Baywatch'. If you are a 40-year-old guy with average size bones and who was only just about OK at sport at school, your subconscious is not going to hype you as the next Hollywood all-action muscle hero!

The image you will have had is of you with a few pounds off – maybe quite a few pounds. You may have seen yourself being happier within situations that are very real and which you can easily relate to . . . playing with your children, being content with your partner, walking along the street and really enjoying walking along the street because your breath isn't coming in laboured gasps any longer. You may see yourself fitting into a lovely dress you bought a couple of years ago, or a pair of jeans that seemed a good idea at the time except that Christmas, or maybe a baby, intervened!

Men seeking their Ideal Weight have to find and discover their own realism. Your subconscious doesn't lie to you. The Ideal You that you are now beginning to envisage is lovely. It is permanent and, very soon, it will be you.

What you saw is what you should become. It is good. It is the real you. There should be no extremes in life. Your Ideal Weight Programme shape, size and figure is ideal to you and you alone. If you still consider – and I know you don't – that supermodels and superhunks are the best role models, then just begin to follow the tales of the commonplace wreckage of their personal lives, which is well documented in the media.

8. *I am learning to love myself because I fully understand that unless I love myself I cannot love others.*

This is a lovely affirmation! I am especially fond of it. In the mid-1960s I lived in India for about six months. It was the place to be at the time. Discovering the belief systems and values of Eastern cultures might have seemed more like a five-minute fad for the pop groups of the time, but it was an exercise of enormous value to those of us who were totally locked into the Western belief systems of the day. Eastern systems such as yoga were emphasizing the vital and primary importance of spiritual and physical well-being. There was a vibrancy and an extremely sensual and sensuous feel to all these new experiences. The country may have been poor, but I found that people were not being actively trained from childhood to feel guilty and introverted!

You will have come across people who always have a vague notion that, somehow, things may start getting better tomorrow. You might even have felt like this yourself. Things will not start getting better unless you do something about it. The Ideal Weight Programme is already doing a great deal to start making things a great deal better.

Think of a moment when you have felt real love. It may be a childhood memory of a parent or relative hugging you tight. It may be the first time you kissed for real. It may be an image of making love with someone you felt, or feel, really close to. Hold that feeling from that special moment. That's how you deserve to feel about yourself all the time. You are worth that loving every day from now on. This is your life here and now . . . this is not a dress re-hearsal for possible better times up ahead.

So, let's play for real by confirming that:

I am learning to love myself because I fully understand that unless I love myself I cannot love others.

9. *From this day onwards I shall become a successful individual. I can achieve my goals. As I think, so I shall become.*

I am not going to bombard you with motivational tirades. I am going to give you a few real examples of the mind-body connection from my own experience.

When I was an undergraduate at the University of London, fellow students and I decided to conduct a little 'experiment' on a particularly boring professor who was due to lecture us on a lovely summer after-noon when we would rather have been elsewhere.

I first bumped into the professor shortly after breakfast and said: 'Good morning, Sir. I hope you are feeling all right because you look very pale today'.

A little while later one of my friends was asked to run an errand for the professor and said: 'Certainly Sir, but could you please just repeat what you said to check I've understood it correctly. Your voice sounds very hoarse. You must be getting a sore throat.'

A second friend made sure he stood near the pro-fessor in the queue for lunch and asked: 'Can I get your food for you, professor? You look a bit unsteady on your feet and maybe you should sit down'.

The afternoon lecture was cancelled. The professor was in bed, running a temperature . . . pure co-incidence?

Let me give you another example. A few years ago there was a case in the US of a remarkable lady who was treating cancer patients diagnosed as terminally ill. The treatment was designed to help the body to fight back.

The key method was to focus on the declining levels of white blood cells as a thriving and rapidly growing shoal of piranha fish and on the growing tumours as hamburger meat.

Extraordinarily, within a few weeks the white blood cell counts of the patients had dramatically increased beyond any normal medical expectations. The tumours had grown smaller.

This is possibly very exceptional. But I can give you another example. A few years ago, a close friend of mine suffered a heart attack while on holiday.

During his recovery in hospital, which he was finding incredibly boring, I went to visit him. I told him the story of the piranhas and the hamburger meat, and I said that I believed he could use this experience to clear the clogged arteries which had brought on the attack.

He was determined to fight back and recover quickly. The Channel Tunnel was just underway, and he had heard of how it was being built using a huge drill at each end, both of them the size of houses and with gigantic diamond-hard edges smashing and grinding their way through solid rock.

He visualized one of those giant drills in each of his arteries and turned them on, making sure they ran twenty-four hours a day, cleaning and scraping out every last ounce of debris.

One month later, back home, he went for a

periodic medical check-up. The doctor could hardly believe he had had such a major attack a month before. In fact, my friend had to produce his medical records to convince him.

To me, these examples prove the power of your mind. Unleashing the power of your subconscious is the key to tackling your overweight problems.

To get a better idea of this yourself, call to mind the biggest cinema complex you have ever seen. It may have half a dozen separate screen theatres, it may even have twenty.

Now imagine a cinema complex that stretches on forever. An infinite number of screen theatres going off over the horizon.

That is what your subconscious mind is like when you set yourself a task – it draws on all its experience . . . and the movie that is playing on each and every one of those screens is directly influencing how you feel at this moment.

In children, the link between the subconscious and conscious minds is particularly direct. If your toddler is stumbling across the stones on the way down to the seaside and you say 'Don't fall over', then it is highly likely that he or she will immediately tumble straight over.

The only way you could have some success in keeping the child upright would have been by using very direct and positive images, such as: 'Be careful, concentrate on your balance, watch exactly where you are putting your feet and move slowly.'

This link fades with age, although we have already done a great deal of work to enable you to make strong connections whenever you choose to.

Let's return to all those streets upon streets of cinemas. The same movie is showing in each and every screen theatre. The star actor is yourself. In fact, you are the only actor. The plot is very simple and very monotonous. You are sitting in one big room, full of cupboards and fridges with glass doors.

Inside all these cupboards and fridges are all the foods you still love . . . the cake, the chocolate, the fizzy pops, the oven chips, the packet pizza, the butter, the bacon etc. And you are sitting there surrounded by all these foods. You have a tray on your knee. On it is the latest diet fad that a supermarket or magazine promotion or a salesman has forced on you.

It might be a bar of imitation chocolate, or a sickly milkshake, or a tiny portion of very plain salad. Whatever it is, it is the only food you are allowed to eat and you don't like it. You are still completely wedded to your old eating regime. The tray on your knees seems completely alien. You have not accepted that this is the new eating habit for you in any way whatsoever.

The tray is saying in a weak voice to you: 'Don't eat the cake, don't eat the chocolate, the fizzy pops, the oven chips, the packet pizza, the butter, the bacon . . . ' And you still love all these foods and you can still see them all.

Just the fact that it is saying these things is enough to make you crave them. Just like the toddler and not falling over, you can't think of 'not' doing something without actually thinking of doing it.

It wouldn't even matter if the tray was shouting at you in a loud voice because you don't like or trust it.

You still like and trust all your old foods and, what is more, not only are they still in sight but they are shouting at you: 'Eat me, eat me, eat me'.

The title of the film could be 'Pressure, Desire, Guilt and Failure: the History of My Dieting by (fill in your own name)'.

Let's just remind ourselves of the affirmation that we are covering:

From this day onwards I shall become a successful individual. I can achieve my goals. As I think I shall become.

Now, there is one very obvious and very simple way to make this come true. We are going to change the film playing in the cinema. This one is called 'Me and My Ideal Weight Programme: My Painless and Permanent Weight Loss by (fill in your name)'.

Moreover, in the current tradition of the really successful movie superstars, you are both the star of the movie and its director. We have already, together, written quite a lot of the outline script and screenplay. Keep focusing on this new film playing on all those screens, and you will find yourself rapidly approaching your Ideal Weight.

10. *I am becoming aware of myself. I have developed control.*

Oh yes! You can be absolutely sure of this one!

A Simple Technique for Life Management

After all that hard work, we are going to do something to help you relax. It won't just help you to relax in the next few minutes, it can help to bring relaxation and control into every day for the rest of your life. Whenever you want a little help, it will be there. I have taught this method to thousands of people – and I have never heard a bad report yet.

Have you ever shaken your fist at someone when you are angry? It's pointless. It confirms and heightens the anger. Instead of letting the anger out, it increases the emotion and the hatred. You will be left, literally, shaking with rage – even if you were not in that severe a state before you raised, tensed and shook your fist, you will be by the time you have finished. It will have really got the adrenalin flowing and, without an outlet – the actual physical fight that your body was being prepared for – those hormones will just rush round your veins.

This is how it works. Think of something or some situation that really annoys you. Like when passing kids ring your doorbell and run off. Or when you rush for a bus and just miss it. Something that happens in your life and something that makes your blood pressure soar. (You are never as vulnerable to unnecessary eating as when your emotions and hormones are careering around all over the place.)

Close your eyes and visualize this annoying situation. You are getting very good at getting in touch with your emotions by now, so recreate that anger and feel it rise up within you.

Now, extend the arm with which you would

naturally make your fist. Straighten that arm and open your hand, palm down.

Grab the situation in your hand. Imagine it. Picture it. Feel it. Clench your fist. Close your eyes and imagine grabbing hold of the entire picture of yourself in whatever situation it was that made you angry. See yourself in that state of annoyance, stress and anger and feel the anguish.

Hold that situation tight in your fist and draw your hand backwards, round and up – as if you were going to shake your fist like you used to.

But don't. Hold the tense situation firmly in your tight fist. Hold your breath as well. You have complete control of whatever it is that usually makes you angry.

Now, straighten your arm suddenly, straightening out your fingers again as you go. Exhale as you do so. Punch the breath out. Blow the problem away.

Picture the situation cascading and crashing away from you out of your open hand. See it hurtling off into the distance with all your stress and anger still in the situation and say out loud, in whatever words come most naturally to you (as strong as you like): 'I don't need this and I don't want it and I am not going to have it any longer!'

As the unpleasant situation is hurled away from you, keep your eyes closed and keep your open palm down to the ground and your arm straightened. But with the situation now completely gone, the tension will immediately ease. But if it doesn't, repeat time and again until it does.

Now, change the picture. Think of a time when you were totally relaxed and happy. Be specific. You might be lying on a beach during your last lovely holiday. Whatever it is, feel the relaxation and the happiness come flooding into the hole from which the unpleasant situation has vanished. The good feelings take over completely and you are totally relaxed. Now, capture those feelings, so that you can recall them whenever you desire instant relaxation. Think of your writing hand. Make the letter 'O' with your thumb and forefinger. Take a deep breath. Hold for a count of four and, as you squeeze your thumb and forefinger, exhale and think, 'Relax'.

Practise these techniques until they work totally for you. These techniques call upon the strongest system of communication ever developed by psychology – based on Neuro Linguistic Programming. You have been experiencing the system's power throughout all of the book so far.

By this stage you are beginning to develop the higher levels of skill in communicating with yourself to be able to master the use of this extremely powerful tool. With practice it will consolidate into a subtle little movement of the hand that instantly turns pain into relaxation.

Use this tool well and it will reward you with the ability to take complete control of situations that previously used to drive you crazy – and straight to the biscuit tin!

4
Food, weight and relationships

People are fat because they are persuaded to stuff more calories down themselves than their bodies need. But there is a host of triggers that sets off this unwelcome behaviour and many of these emanate from close to home – in fact, from the home where you grew up as a child.

'You've done so well, why don't you have a lettuce salad?'

'Who's a good little girl? Have a carrot!'

Do these statements make a complete mockery of your usual patterns of thought association? Most people are more used to a rather different reward system. In most people's values, chocolate and biscuits would come naturally to mind – and junk food forever becomes associated with pain relief and pleasure.

Human kind is unique in the animal world in the degrees of tuition that we offer to our children in the rearing process. Feeding one's children is instinctive on the part of both the mother and the father. It is an extremely strong instinct, deeply locked into our priorities for our offspring's survival.

This is why it seems so cute when we see parent birds feeding their tiny chicks, or a cat suckling her tiny kittens, or a huge and powerful tigress carefully tearing up little morsels of meat for her cubs. It is an instinct for which we feel the deepest sympathy and these are acts that evoke strong but tender emotions within us.

But, within the animal kingdom, the offspring usually quickly go their own way when they have grown big and strong enough and mastered the fundamentals of feeding themselves.

Mummy tigresses do not threaten their cubs with the withholding of favourite foods if they fail to concentrate on their homework.

No, man is unique. On top of all the desperately confusing images and pressures already surrounding the issue of food, we heap on our children a whole extra pile of food-related values that have absolutely nothing to do with nutrition. Families, while they can bring huge joy and comfort, are equally capable of making you fat.

Hug them, don't force feed them

It starts from the youngest age. The baby is crying. Does its nappy need changing? No. Is it cold? No. Is it uncomfortable? No. We go through a checklist and rapidly eliminate all the possible causes of the infant's distress and narrow the likely cause down to hunger.

The baby is breast fed or enjoys a bottle and the crying stops. The baby is happy again . . . and we are satisfied that we have fed our much loved little boy or girl.

The pattern of pacifying a child with food is set deeply in us. And because a child is with a parent through a much longer and more detailed developmental stage than is common in the animal kingdom, it is the first of many behavioural functions that food assumes between parent and child.

How many times have you been in a supermarket and seen a toddler crying while sitting in its pram, only to be pacified with a biscuit, or a piece or chocolate?

From a parent's point of view there is nothing simpler than placing the biscuit or chocolate into the child's hand. It gives a few minutes respite while trying to continue with the shopping. It is a hassle to undo all the baby's straps, pacify it with love, put it back and do up all the straps again while trying to do your shopping in a busy store, particularly if you are on your own. But the process is strongly bonding junk food to two extremely commonplace desires – comfort on the part of the infant and a little peace and quiet on the part of the parent.

As the child begins to grow a little older, it is just as likely that the parents will start, probably completely unconsciously, to use food as a means of more complex behavioural influence. It is an accepted part of toilet training that if the child successfully completes its mission in the toilet and not in his or her pants, then some form of a reward should be offered. That reward is often a sweet.

Then the parent wants to consolidate the achievement and looks for motivation towards a continuation of the breakthrough. So, what is the child told? 'Next time you go to the toilet, Mummy will give you a lollipop.'

This kind of motivation – giving a treat for accomplishment – is forging an unnecessary and potentially dangerous emotional connection with food. A sweet food treat is very poor indeed, but any associations with food in these contexts is bad enough. My examples at the start of this section, involving vegetables, were not appropriate either – they were merely to highlight the complete acceptance and complacency surrounding this very serious topic.

There are many things that a parent should give to a child and, as a father myself, I wholeheartedly agree that it is an absolute joy to give them. These things include love (number one, offer it frequently and in bucketfuls), comfort, encouragement, guidance, friendship, approval and time. To deny a child any of these things – and plenty of things that I have not included – is to deprive and starve them.

But be aware that food is a great and powerful instrument of the parent. 'Finish everything on your plate . . . there are starving children in India . . . waste not, want not . . . food costs money.'

There are common and specific uses of this instrument: 'You are a very, very naughty child. No supper for you tonight unless you do as you are told.' (Here the parent is punishing the child by depriving, or threatening to deprive it, of food. It is building anxiety into the eating process.)

'If you behave yourself, I will buy you an ice-cream later.' (Food being used as a bribe.)

'You did so well in school that I am going to take you out to your favourite burger restaurant and you can order whatever you want.' (Food being used as a reward.)

'So Mummy's little baby isn't feeling too good. OK, go to bed and I'll bring you a nice big plateful of one of your extra special favourites.' (Food being used as a comfort.)

'I'm so sorry that your pet died. Let's go into the kitchen and I'll do us a smashing great dish of spaghetti. That will take your mind off it and make the tears go away.' (Food being used as a pain remover.)

'Oh dear. That's a nasty bruise you've got on your knee. I know, a nice chocolate bar will make it better. (Food being used as a healer.)

There are others. I am sure you have heard them. You may have used them yourself. Don't. I have stressed that there are no lists of banned foods in this book and there are no lists of recommended recipes. There will be plenty of suggestions but no orders – the choice will always remain yours. But when it comes to the mental ABUSE of food, there are some very clear instructions from the Ideal Weight Programme . . . don't!

There are many, many ways of disciplining (not for one minute am I suggesting that you abandon the food handcuffs just to let the little devils run wild), motivating, comforting, showing disapproval and of praising your children – but food should never, under any circumstances, be used as a tool.

Hugs and kisses are a marvellous tool. The occasional book or constructive toy makes an excellent tool. Making a special reward such as a bike ride in

the park contingent upon certain and satisfactory behaviour is an excellent mechanism for both
motivation and discipline. But a bar of chocolate is
not a tool and neither is a slice of wholemeal bread.

In becoming parents we take on a vast variety of responsibilities. Hopefully our children will grow up to
be happy, productive, fulfilled and healthy. It is not
our responsibility to make them fat. If we do so, they
will generally be unhealthier, unhappier, have less
fulfilled lives – and die younger.

The mysterious case of one girl's weight problem

As we have already seen and discussed, the programming of our children towards unwanted food
associations and eventual fatness comes in many
guises. One of the weirdest cases that I have ever en-
countered left me completely baffled.

In the 1970s, while I was running a weight clinic
session in Hawaii, a couple brought their daughter,
who was eleven or twelve, to see me. She had three
older sisters but was the only child who was overweight.

The little girl did not have a particularly large build
but she was carrying a serious amount of fat. I talked
with the parents at length. They were big-boned and
serious people, of East European descent and they
seemed unlikely types to be over-indulging their offspring with junk and sweets. And I learned that the
family did eat relatively well-balanced meals, even if

they were tending to emphasize meat and dairy produce too much. Trashy treats were not on the agenda.

The little girl herself appeared totally normal and happy. She showed no indications of any tendencies towards cravings or binges to make up for any deficiencies in her home or school life. She was also keen on sport and took plenty of exercise. A recent check-up by her physician confirmed that she was in fine health with no hormonal or other growth abnormalities.

I was stumped. I called in a female colleague for a second opinion. She spotted a clue that I would never have noticed.

The little girl was well-dressed, but in fashions, when my attention was drawn to it, that were a good few years out of date. My colleague and I made an appointment to visit the otherwise happy family in their own home.

We found that there was a considerable age gap between the three elder girls and their little sister. They had all left home by then, either to go to college or get married.

We looked at some photographs of them. They were pretty girls and big, tall and strong in that way that many younger Americans area. Then the penny – or the cent – dropped. The fat little girl had always been wearing hand-me-downs!

The parents were not being unkind. Far from it . . . the youngest girl had always been immaculately dressed but she had subconsciously always been struggling to fill up the clothes she was given. She had a much smaller frame than her bigger sisters, but fat was doing the filling-up. Her mind had constantly been guiding her body to eat bigger portions at meal-times so that her size could match her clothing!

The trio dropped by to see me about a year later. The daughter was looking very pretty in the latest summer fashion, which was showing off her much slimmer figure. That, to me, has to be the ultimate instant proof of how our mind controls how our body looks.

I could continue developing the Ideal Weight Programme for the next 100 years and I would never have resolved that particular weight problem unaided!

But there are several typical fat/emotion relationships that I have witnessed on a regular basis for several decades – and, no doubt, I shall continue to encounter them for the rest of my working life.

We stuff their emotions and they stuff their faces

In our societies children are not taught healthy ways to release their emotions. We are often taught – usually by example – destructive ways such as screaming and shouting. As we discovered in building up your competence in 'Making the Letter O', these methods do not in fact release the emotion. They just amplify the emotion and often end up by hurting someone else as well.

Or we are taught to repress our emotions. We are given a lot of 'don't feel' messages as we grow. These 'don't feel' messages often depend on which sex you are. Boys are not allowed to feel sad or scared. Have you ever heard anyone speaking like this: 'Come on, be a big boy, don't cry. Big boys don't cry!'

What are we teaching little boys when we speak to them in this manner? We are teaching them to stuff, or hide, their emotions. We do similar things to our little girls but under a slightly different guise.

It is fine for little girls to cry we think. After all, they are soft . . . and if they are not, many parents make absolutely sure that they become soft and highly vulnerable to being hurt.

But they are not allowed to become angry. It is 'not lady-like'. Little girls, of course, are supposed to be sugar (!) and spice and all things nice, and both boys and girls are to be seen and not heard. All these absurd and destructive messages are demands that children must not be themselves. We are systematically teaching them to lie and to put on acts. We are teaching them to repress their true feelings. But there is a direct line between unexpressed emotion, the tension it creates and deviant behaviour – which includes the needless and regular ingestion of large quantities of junk food.

Children are greatly aided in their learning process of how to 'stuff our feelings' by watching the example of the grown-ups around them. They pass on their compulsive habits to the next generation.

Many people with weight problems often also have other psychological problems. Alcohol, or drugs, or cigarettes, or food are universally used to stuff down feelings. Every time one of the 'don't feel' emotions comes along, people reach out for their packeted and bottled feeling-stuffers. Alcohol and binge eating go straight to your waistline. All these feeling-stuffers, by various rates, accelerate the speed at which you grow old and die.

The more emotions you have to repress, the more feeling-stuffers it takes to do so. The more frequently you use them, the greater dose you have to use. The old image of the happy fat person is almost invariably a cover-up.

The weight we carry from childhood

Many children experience traumas that they find extremely difficult to cope with. I am going to touch on the main categories.

The first is unresolved pain. Small children are very sensitive creatures. They are also very perceptive and intuitive. They can feel emotions such as pain and fear from the adults around them but there is very little they can do to deal with these powerful and often frightening feelings. Something they can do however is to shelter within excessive eating.

The second is emotional abuse. Some parents take out their fear and anger and pain on their children. It is distressingly common that frustrations are vented on the young. The child may represent and highlight all the things that the parent resents in himself or herself and this may come out as emotional abuse. Criticisms, put downs and name-calling may be used to 'discipline' the child.

All forms of abuse greatly affect the self-esteem of the child. If you were abused as a child, you may find yourself engaged in all manner of self-destructive behaviour because, underneath, you may really hate yourself. I frequently encounter such problems. If our parents did not like us, it may be difficult for us to like ourselves, which is everybody's birthright and one of the cornerstones of a happy life. The Ideal Weight Programme is deeply concerned with these feelings and with how, correctly, to learn how to love yourself.

The next category is physical abuse and usually involves the parent releasing his or her anger on the child. This, too, is usually done in the name of 'discipline'. It causes the child to fear and hate the parent. The child has many feelings which must be repressed – turned inwards on him or herself. Feelings of anxiety can sometimes be traced back to physical abuse.

Neglect comes in many forms and degrees. Like all forms of abuse, it can occur to children of any social class. A very common form is where both parents are out working long hours. This may happen because both parents are in low-paid work and are having great trouble making ends meet. It can also occur where neither partner is prepared to abandon a high-flying career for the sake of child rearing.

It can also happen in households where the parents came from austere 'Victorian' families themselves and it is simply the acquired habit to pay little attention to children.

Maybe, even, the parents remember when times were really bad and there wasn't enough money, and so they carry on working all the hours they can simply as an ongoing and automatic safety mechanism.

You may go back to your own childhood and think that it was pretty good and pretty normal. That may well be totally true. But a degree of emptiness that has always been filled with food may often be hard to identify: there are many people who will begin to eat as soon as they walk into their own homes. This often goes back to households where food was a substitute for missing love.

Then there is sexual abuse. Some estimates put the levels as high as one in six of women and one in eleven of men who have been sexually abused as a child. You may wonder what this has to do with being overweight – but it has everything to do with it. Often the 'child part' of a subconscious mind will make the decisions that guide a person for the rest of their life. From about the age of six months onwards, the subconscious is a gigantic and complete storehouse of everything that ever happens to you. Somewhere, sitting on one of the countless shelves, is every event and the emotions that accompanied it.

An example of an early decision out of the subconscious would be: 'If I am fat, then no one will bother me (sexually) again. It will stop it happening any more because I will be fat and ugly.' Experience of working with adults who were sexually abused as youngsters has proven this often to be the case.

They may also gain weight because they are stuffing their feelings about the abuse. You see, gaining weight is a very common reaction to any traumatic event.

Typical of such an event may be loss of someone close. Grief is an emotion that is habitually and culturally stuffed back down. 'Be strong', 'bear up', 'be brave' and 'time will heal' would be examples of 'don't feel' commands from this kind of distressing situation. And rather than allow a healthy outlet for that emotion, many people will turn to food for consolation.

Beware! Your partner can make you fat

You might have an insecure partner, or relative, within your home, or your immediate circle of influence, and it is important to recognize how this can unknowingly hinder your progress – or even sabotage your efforts to lose weight.

You may constantly be trying to rescue this person through failure, not just in the Ideal Weight Programme but in many areas of your life. A husband may have subconsciously been guided towards marrying a fat woman because he thought that there would be no threat from competing males – or vice versa.

As the overweight partner starts to lose weight, obstacles might well be placed in his or her way, such as statements like 'Don't bother, I love you just as you are', or in the form of boxes of chocolates, cans of beer, or tubs of ice-cream. It is important that a more stable basis for the relationship can be worked out. It is everyone's right to be slim and healthy.

Or people can see the passion and excitement receding from their initially fulfilling togetherness . . . children, the struggle to pay the mortgage, the everyday monotony can all seem a million years removed from mad, passionate honeymoon lovemaking. Enter food as the consolation.

Then there is the lovemaking itself. A man may want sex, a woman may crave togetherness. They may clash and the stand-off tensions can be stuffed down in the time-honoured traditions of emotionally driven eating.

The Ideal Weight Programme does not create problems but it does highlight where existing problems have taken control of your eating habits. By being aware of what these difficulties might be, it allows you to take preventive and curative measures from this moment onwards. By permanently and painlessly resolving your weight problems, you may also have the opportunity to tackle other negative and restrictive influences within your life. There are many more than the few I have listed. As I have already noted, psychologists, by the very nature of our jobs, have a tendency to err towards a morbid outlook. The important point is that this programme is giving you the ability to get in touch with what is important to you and to identify your own guiding influences. What is more, you are gradually being provided with a powerful, and comprehensive toolkit to be able to put together the you that you wish to be.

Why won't my weight go down?

You may find yourself reaching a plateau within your progress through the Ideal Weight Programme. You gradually and painlessly and permanently reduce to a certain level, which just seems a modest distance along the course of your overall journey, only to find yourself stuck fast.

You need to ask yourself what dipping below what is only one tiny milestone means to you. Certain weights mean certain things to certain people.

I once had a lady patient in her mid-thirties who came to me privately at my clinic for advice on weight loss. She was not particularly overweight – she weighed about eleven and a half stone and wanted to get down to ten stone, which she felt was her Ideal Weight – the size she had been as a teenager.

She had tried numerous approaches to dieting. She could lose weight and she even had the willpower to keep most of it off (she had for a long period been nearer thirteen stone) but she simply hit a wall at ten-and-a-half stone. There seemed to her to be no reason for it because she did not feel that she was forcing her weight down excessively at this level.

I found out, through counselling, that she had been sexually molested when she was 17 by her mother's second husband, her stepfather. She told her mother about the attack. The reply was devastating: 'If you hadn't made yourself out to be so attractive and sexy this would never have happened. You've ruined my relationship.'

It transpired that my patient had never been able to sustain a fulfilling long-term relationship. Her mother's vicious and thoughtless comments had taught the daughter to associate herself and her sexuality with assault and failed relationships.

We worked together and, I am delighted to re-count, the lady not only made – and kept to – her Ideal Weight, but began to heal a very old wound.

That meant a great deal more to her than just pounds, as you can appreciate.

Of course, this is a very severe trauma case. But we have already discovered the insecurity of spouses, partners and relatives, not to mention the other friends and acquaintances whose opinions you are used to respecting, and how this affects your weight control. It is this insecurity of others than can keep you stuck on a plateau.

Do you still want to be fat?

Another reason for reaching a plateau could be summarized by the simple expression 'too much, too soon'. As I said very clearly earlier in this book, there is no way that this course will work if I simply sent out course tapes to everyone in the world who wants to lose weight. A map is not the journey, just as a menu is not a meal.

There is more to the Ideal Weight Club than simply plugging in your stereo headphones and taking a short time-out in your hectic schedule!

But, I am sure that by getting this far, you have been thinking about all the points that we are discussing. You have been interacting with your Affirmations and delighting in the exploding powers of your visualization. And you have been constantly reflecting in the knowledge that it is not YOU who made you overweight and it is not YOU who had previously struggled for a painless and permanent way forward. The knowledge and the resources are building. They are strong in you by now.

Beating those Plateaux

Use this worksheet to take stock about why you don't seem to be moving any closer to your Ideal Weight, if that is a problem at the moment. There are no correct answers, but asking yourself these questions should spur you on!

What does attaining your Ideal Weight mean to you?

_____

How long ago would it be when you were your Ideal Weight?

_____

When on a past diet, what weight could you not get below?

_____

Have you any fears concerning reaching your Ideal Weight?

_____

How would you feel if by magic you could wake up in the morning at your Ideal Weight?

_____

When did you last feel like that?

_____

What were your circumstances at that time?

_____

Change should be fun. Change is good!

The true meaning of stress has nothing to do with the totally achievement-oriented ideas that modern society has given it. Stress is not really about driving a Formula One racing car. Neither is it really about standing up at a stockbroker's trading desk, red braces straining over hand-made shirts, shouting buy and sell orders for the Japanese yen. That isn't stress by its proper meaning, that's pressure.

Stress is the body's reaction to change. Moving from a house where you have lived for many years to a new home is likely to be significantly more stressful than suffering a car crash. The latter will break bones, cause concussion and take time to heal from. It may lead to anxieties when driving again and particularly strong anxieties when associated with the circumstances of the crash – the location, the weather conditions, the reason for your journey I have quite recently had just these experiences with a car crash. But the primary emotion is not stress.

Moving home when you are very locked into one location is very stressful. It is a change that you experience very intensively, as a lot of our most valuable time is spent at home.

Changing the shape and composition of your body is something that you experience even more intensively. It is a huge change and, as we have just established, change is stress. We have discovered that the mind controls the body. The body is the home of the mind. Totally reshaping that home is therefore by its nature very stressful. But the Ideal Weight Programme is very careful to alert and condition the mind to the new and exciting reality that its living circumstances are about to change – for the better – and it will love its new environment!

Our range of tools is growing rapidly but let's now return to the real workhorses of the programme.

The Affirmations

When we first did our Affirmations together, only just a very short while ago, they seemed somewhat alien and irrelevant to you. That has quickly changed as meanings hugely relevant to your life have been awoken and then anchored in your mind by them. The changed perspectives that are constructing your own and personal Ideal Weight Programme have also been locked into place by the Affirmations.

This time when we do our Affirmations we are going to take a little time, so take it easy. This is the moment to reflect and recap, after the huge volume of data we have discussed so far, on all that we have achieved up to now.

We have spent a great deal of effort knocking things down. Most of the rest of this book is going to be concerned with building things up. The most important item by far on this agenda is you.

We will follow the Affirmations with some fun and easy visualization exercises that will underline and consolidate your new levels of focused competence in painlessly and permanently losing weight. If you have pen and paper, let's begin. Remember to write each of these out.

1. *I can lose weight easily.*

One day at a time. So effortlessly that no one, least of all yourself, even notices what is going on.

2. *I can easily lose weight simply by the changing of my eating habits and they will become permanent.*

I would imagine that you have felt shocked, annoyed even, as you have begun to appreciate fully that the last person in the whole world, until now, who has had any meaningful input into your eating habits has been you. What you put into your own mouth is your business, not what big business, or history, or your family, or me, or whoever, decides for you.

3. *From now on I will incorporate a very simple activity programme, be it walking, swimming, or whatever.*

If you have ached after aerobics, been in agony from athletics, felt wasted from weights or got the jitters from the very mention of jogging, then writing out this Affirmation at first must have seemed as attractive as signing a contract for your first professional boxing contest! Relax, we will deal with the issue of little activity in due course. There is an expression that goes 'Don't run before you can walk'. We will be going further than that and not running at all!

4. *Because I love myself, from now on I will choose healthy and nutritious food.*

And what foods are they? When is he going to tell me what they are? Where are the recipes and the lists and the latest obscure combination of foodstuffs that he must have for us? . . . You're in the wrong book for all of that, as you will probably have realized by now.

   You know what you should eat. You know it in

detail and you know it for a fact. It is just that everything we have detailed has not allowed you the
scope, nor the confidence, to access this knowledge.

Much of the food in our shops is shamefully adul-
terated rubbish. Our conception of food and our
relationship with it is a total perversion.

Water has rapidly gone the same way. Chemical
additives spoil the quality of much of the product
itself. Children associate drinking with sugar-laden
syrups. Millions of adults extremely rarely drink anything except tea, coffee and alcohol.

The Ideal Weight Programme is teaching you how
to be in touch with yourself and how to love yourself.
It will also show you the full and surprising extent of
your existing knowledge of food and, perhaps, help
you to fill in a few blank areas.

5. *I am responsible for me. I am responsible for my body and
I am responsible for the food that I eat.*

Do you remember the blindfold that you used to
wear? Do you recall that we threw it away for good a
couple of chapters ago?

6. *From now on I will be able to control and express my
emotions.*

Read this paragraph and then close your eyes. Drift
across all the pages of this book so far, just as an ice
skater on a frozen lake elegantly circles and crosses
over all the parts of the ice. Take your time, there is
no rush. You will stop at a point where you felt a
strong emotion emerge from something that you

read. Pick up the experience and the emotion and open your eyes and write it down.

That's good. I am not going to test you in any way on this. The experience and the emotion are your own. The way you plucked them out of your subconscious is just one little bit of evidence of how you are developing the tools to be totally and independently responsible for yourself because you are learning how to find and identify your emotions.

7. From now on, I will start to achieve and maintain a healthy shape, size and figure – the shape and size I would like to be.

Close your eyes and draw up that picture of the ideal you again. It's not a fantasy out of the pages of a glossy magazine. It's you and you love the idea that it will soon be you.

8. I am learning to love myself because I fully understand that unless I love myself I cannot love others.

We talked at length about the 'don't feel' commands and the repressed pressure and problems that they inevitably create. Most people would be incapable of being able to relate to the concept of 'loving oneself'. Their thought associations might vary from pure vanity to furtive masturbation.

But do you remember that lovely warm feeling that we brought back when we thought of laughing, hugging, kissing, togetherness and making love? That emotion is the object of loving oneself. As we have said, it is your birthright to own and to recall on demand whenever you wish.

9. *From this day onwards I shall become a successful individual. I can achieve my goals. As I think, so I shall become.*

Remember that we have been writing a movie script together in which you are both the star actor and the director? Remember, also, the horror movie that we have changed and got rid of – the one of the madness of all your previous dieting experiences? This script for your Ideal Programme doesn't have any no's or can't's in it. Have you noticed that? You probably haven't because it is a very simple task to banish failure-speak from one's life.

The Ideal Weight Programme does not ask: 'What's the matter with you?' We are not in the business of making the presumption that anything is the matter. If we ever do that, then as sure as anything, something very quickly will be the matter. You will have to create problems to relate to the question. No, the Ideal Weight Programme is in the business of helping you decide exactly where you want to be and then helping you to get there. Does that make sense? It is likely to be an important breakthrough from the failure-speak that may have been guiding you from birth.

All our Affirmations are very positive and they lead you to visualize positive actions in process. Importantly, all this progress is very relevant, realistic and achievable.

Recently, a lady came to see me at my clinic. We

discussed her Ideal Weight objectives and she told me that she wished to lose three-and-a-half stones. That seemed like a realistic goal and we talked some more.

I asked her why she had a large suitcase with her and her reply was 'I'm getting married tomorrow and I need to lose all this weight quickly!'

You may laugh but many people's dieting goals are just as unrealistic, if less obviously so. We have discussed the pressure of role models that is heaped upon us – the supermodels and superhunks.

But another huge area of attempted goals being miles wide of the target would be the whole concept of New Year resolutions. It is 11.55pm on New Year's Eve. You have had quite a lot to drink and everyone is singing along and having a grand old time.

'Next year I am not going to be so fat and lazy,' you whisper to yourself and then plunge back into the party atmosphere. Ever been there? The 'goal' is negative, it is unspecific, it is not focused, it is not the produce of a serious discussion with your subconscious.

Successful people don't just mutter half-hearted desires under their breath, only for the whispered words to be blown away with the next event or emotion. Successful people take risks and they turn failure into a learning experience. By being on the Ideal Weight Programme you have refused to retreat inwards into failure.

I am gratified that you have taken a risk on me and I hope that this intense learning process has already washed away the pain of all previous dieting fiascos. In place of that past pain there is increasing joy and the thrill of the anticipation of the good things to come.

10. *I am becoming aware of myself. I have developed control.*

The following exercises will confirm that you have progressed to a new level of control.

BEING IN TOUCH – AND IT FEELS GOOD
Your subconscious mind knows a great deal more about your Ideal Weight than any diet chart, graph or tables can ever know. It will even know a great more than your own doctor.

I told you at the beginning of this book that we don't use scales in the Ideal Weight Programme. However, I want you to imagine a set of scales. These imaginary scales are the only ones you will ever use on the programme. Imagine those big old-fashioned ones with the large round face – the type you sometimes get in railway stations, or shopping centres.

When this paragraph is finished, close your eyes and complete this remarkable exercise. Imagine that you are in a very tall shopping centre. In fact, there are ten flights of escalators before you get down to the basement where you need to be. You go slowly down each flight. It is a very elegant shopping centre. The lights are soft and welcoming. The music is pleasant and soothing and the air conditioning is fresh and calming. Go down each of the ten flights slowly. Breathe in as you go down each flight and breathe out at the bottom of each one, counting down as you breathe out . . . ten, nine, eight, keeping track as we descend each escalator . . . all the way down until you come to the basement. In the basement are some of those big public weighing scales. You want to get on because you have reached your Ideal Weight and you want to see it up on the big scales – and you want anyone else who is passing to see it as well because you have reached your realistic Ideal Weight and you know you will stay there easily. Go slowly down the ten flights of escalators now, remembering to count and breathe and then stand on the scales and weigh yourself.

STEPPING INTO THE CIRCLE OF EXCELLENCE

Did you go down the escalator? Did you stand on the scales? What weight did you see? That is your Ideal Weight.

Now, let's go one step nearer that Ideal Weight. This time we are going to be standing up when we do the exercise. So, as usual, go through this rehearsal with me and then close your eyes and do it. Look about two feet in front of you. Mentally draw a circle on the floor. It is the size of the platform on the big old-fashioned weighing scales. See the shape of the platform, its size and its appearance; it is silver-grey metal. This is the Circle of Excellence. Now, remember how you were absolutely bursting with pride. You deserved to feel like this because you have achieved your realistic and permanent Ideal Weight. You are delighted because the process was painless and you know that it will be just as easy to stay there. You are as happy as you could possibly be and you want to step on to those scales and you don't care who sees your weight because it is great. Now, close your eyes, see the platform, see the scales, step on to the platform, admire your Ideal Weight and the new you. It feels great. Do it and feel the picture.

No more weighing scales for you – you don't need them anymore.

5
Why people should stop being fat

In the Introduction, I mentioned the health warnings that public health authorities now insist are prominently placed on cigarette packets and advertisements – bald statements such as 'smokers die younger' and 'smokers are more likely to suffer lethal diseases'. Yet as we see all around us, people still smoke despite these instructions.

But smoking, like eating patterns, is a matter of habit. So far, in the context of food, we have covered extensively the issues of habit-forming pressures and we have looked at them under the numerous guises in which they bombard us.

Something we have touched on is the highly specialized task of changing habit patterns and belief systems. We have now done a great deal of work together on changing your entire relationship with the food you eat.

You have already accomplished more than your old dieting regimes could have taught you in an entire lifetime and you will feel the new powers of control and choice growing strongly within you.

The Ideal Weight Programme always emphasizes the issue of choice because, as we shall discuss in more detail later, there is a strong natural resistance to unsolicited and undesired pressure.

But this chapter's intention is to explicitly introduce the concept of communication – a direct process of communication that can ensure the success of your Ideal Weight Programme. Nowhere am I giving you instructions. You are taking the information that I am enjoying providing for you and you are making up your own mind.

Just as with all the previous diets you have tried – and plenty of the advice may have been perfectly sound – so the smoker does not ignore the honest and well-intentioned warnings of the public health officials.

We don't deliberately ignore people when they point out the undesirable but scientifically-proven outcomes of certain strategies of behaviour.

These outcomes – obesity, heart disease, lung cancer, whatever – are entirely predictable. The problem lies in the fact that these are not being communicated with our belief systems. They are not getting through to us and, if they are not getting through to us, they have no chance of changing us.

I will illustrate all this with an example from my own experience. I smoked for many years. I started as a student in the 1940s. Most of my generation smoked, so there was considerable peer pressure. Then there was the influence that is still instrumental in making many children take up smoking today –

many adults smoked. Kids imitate their parents because they want both to be like them and liked by them.

The promotion of cigarettes in those days was particularly cunning as well. It locked in smoking from generation to generation. The packets had collectable cards in them – great football players of the day, race-horses, steam trains, animals etc. The parents could partly feel they were buying the cigarettes for their children's sake, for the fun associated with the cards. And the children learnt from a young age to be excited by the purchase of cigarettes.

All this was long before anyone even began to consider any possible health risks from the habit. The manufacturers – and the smokers – simply did not have that as an issue to consider.

As a student I used to love to socialize. London, not long after the Second World War, with all the hopes of a new world, was a tremendously exciting place to be. We smoked and exchanged cigarettes while we chatted and swapped dreams in cafés and bars as the city was being rebuilt around us.

I was studying hard, sometimes late at night. I felt the cigarettes helped me to concentrate and stay awake. Then I started doing my lectures and later my stage shows. I can remember the stress relief after some of those early shows as I lit up my first cigarette for more than two hours!

I could go on and quote another dozen or so experiences and emotions that became directly linked between my subconscious and smoking. But we already have more than enough – excitement, happiness, anticipation, youth, discovery, support, relief –

a little packetful of my best friends and the strongest supporters I could ever need.

Then came the Sixties and the first rumours of ill-health associated with smoking. These were followed in the Seventies by reams of statistics and evidence, tales of deaths in numbers to make the history of warfare pale by comparison.

But all these stores might as well have been written in Chinese as far as I was concerned. They were irrelevant to my experience, and an assault on my friends and supporters.

Then my daughter Katie Jane was born. My wife said to me: 'Paul, I wish you would stop smoking. I want her to know you as she is growing up.'

I thought about it. I instantly associated smoking with not seeing my beautiful daughter growing up. I reframed the desire into a positive format: 'I am enjoying my beautiful daughter and I will continue to enjoy her by breathing only clean air.'

I stopped smoking immediately and it has never been an issue for me again because my daughter is beautiful. I am not being self-congratulatory or sanctimonious. This is as important a lesson as this book can teach you. What any human being can achieve through proper communication with his or her mind, any other human being can also achieve. It is only a matter of talking to yourself in the right language. This is what this book has been teaching you to do from the very first page.

Why I should stop being fat

So, we have reframed the question. It is no longer a question of why 'people' should stop being fat; it is now a question of why *you* should stop being fat.

But that question is still not very good, either. The question we are going to be asking from now on is 'What am I going to enjoy about being slim, about being my Ideal Weight?

We have established your lists of the good reasons why you are going to be slim earlier in this book. Refresh your memory as to what they were. Remember that we went over them to make sure that they were framed as positives, to make sure that they weren't just negatives.

Have a look at them again and make some alterations if necessary. We are doing all this by stages. That way there is no shock and you get to understand the process fully. Once you have this process, you have it forever.

By now, it should not be a case of 'when I am no longer fat, I will no longer have my ankles swelling up because I am so heavy'. That will have become 'when I am slim, I am going to enjoy walking around town each and every day'.

Check that you understand what we have done together. You now have your Ideal Weight Programme forever with you and we will now begin to turn it on at full power . . .

The health that matters most is my own health

Ireland, where I live, is rapidly becoming a country of fat people and this is leading to a substantial increase in the rates of cancer, heart disease and other diseases. Six out of ten Irish men are overweight and, according to a medical report published just over a year ago, even just 25lbs excess weight can cut life expectancy by twenty years.

As for Irish obesity rates, it has also been authoritatively and recently reported that 10 percent of all men are obese, and 15 percent of women. The country's leading heart specialists believe that the nation's main killer diseases are largely the result of relative affluence and unhealthy living, which includes a lack of physical activity.

These statistics are repeated throughout the Western world. Furthermore, large-scale research in the US has suggested that the 'yo-yo' pattern of failed dieting – the behaviour which may well have drawn you towards the unique approach of the Ideal Weight Programme – may in itself be a serious health risk.

In a Harvard University study of nearly 8,000 men, those whose weight varied the least between the times they were weighed – in 1962, 1966 and 1977 – had the lowest death rates. Any meaningful weight change, up or down, significantly raised the risk of dying from heart disease.

There is a distinct grey area between the degree of damage caused by the content of diets and the level of harm directly attributable to the degree of obesity itself. But researchers are broadly agreed about certain things; it is only the matter of degree that is in doubt.

The first one is that damage increases as the levels of overweight increase. This is especially true with individuals who have a family history of heart disease or diabetes, or who have high blood pressure. Heart disease, high blood pressure, diabetes and gall bladder disease are specific and serious conditions from which overweight people are more likely to suffer.

At this stage we are down to personal priorities, or, as we have so far labelled these situations, choices. As I said, the first twenty years of horror stories about smoking might for me just as well as have been written in Chinese. For you, the last few pages might just as well have been written in Double Dutch for all the changes this information will make to your eating habits.

The thought of dying young or developing diabetes might trouble you. It might create tension and then anxiety – and what happens then? You do what you have always done. You go to the cupboard or the fridge and pull out a portion of your favourite comforter.

Extra guilt will be created but the central message of this book is that guilt is strictly irrelevant to this situation. You should not hold yourself guilty because you had absolutely no choice in the matter – it hurt, so you ate. It was a 100 percent programmed response. I'll explain more about this later.

But the key issue is whether there is anything that may be of superior value to you than your continuing health-threatening state of overweight. Of course, there must be. Otherwise you would not be following this course. This point is worth making. It is to prove to you that your fat is useless to you as fat. It has another purpose. In psychology this kind of purpose is known as a 'secondary gain'.

If the fat was of overwhelming and unshakeable value to you as fat alone, then you would not be looking to diet. As we have established very thoroughly, that fat is there for some other function, and we now have the strength and sense of direction to start on its permanent removal.

Looking to the future

What is worth the most to you in life? What would you lose if your life were dramatically curtailed, or if you lived in only substantially reduced health?

Do you have children. Will you ever want to have children? Do you have a partner? Do you have any interesting hobbies, jobs or interests? Focus on whatever it is that comes to mind. Close your eyes in a little while and see yourself enjoying being with whoever it is, or doing whatever it is that you enjoy. It does not even have to be anything or anyone that yet exists. It could be something you have always promised yourself that you would do. First see yourself in that situation now. You are overweight and you are enjoying yourself hugely. Then see yourself several years into the future. You are slim and you are enjoying yourself more than you could ever imagine. Hold that situation and simply enjoy those emotions for a while.

Now write down on a piece of paper: '*I look forward to when I am slimmer and healthier so that I can enjoy (write in the experience) even more, and I will enjoy (write it down again) for even longer.*'

Keep this sheet of paper safe. Read it from time to time over the coming months. Close your eyes and see that activity which makes you so happy and feel those gorgeous emotions come flooding back. Remembering this you will no longer endanger yourself by being overweight.

The Affirmations

You will have felt your ability to visualize growing strongly during the book. The Affirmations are now bursting with positive and healthy images of the new you in partnership with the Ideal Weight Programme. You are going to copy them out again in a minute but first I would like you to do something. Take any occasion from the book so far when I have asked you to visualize yourself in a situation and you have felt strong but comforting emotions flood in. Do that now. That is how powerful your Ideal Weight Programme has become. Go through the Affirmations now. Reflect for a couple of minutes after each one – or for as long as you want to – and let the good associations come tumbling out to help you.

1. *I can easily lose weight.*

2. *I can easily lose weight simply by changing my eating habits and these will become permanent.*

3. *From now on I will incorporate a very simple activity programme into my life, be it walking, swimming, or whatever.*

4. *Because I love myself, from now on I will choose healthy and nutritious food.*

5. *I am responsible for me. I am responsible for my body and I am responsible for the food that I eat.*

6. *From now on I will be able to control and express my emotions.*

7. *From now on, I will start to achieve and maintain my healthy shape, size and figure – the shape and size I would like to be.*

8. *I am learning to love myself because I fully understand that unless I love myself I can't love others.*

9. *From this day onwards I shall become a successful individual. As I think, so I shall become.*

10. *I am becoming aware of myself. I have developed control.*

6

You already know what's good for you!

Many readers of this book will know a great deal more about nutrition than I do. After all, food has been a lifelong obsession for them! The vast majority of people who become locked into the obsessive cycle of failed dieting do not have an eating disorder. Far from it – they have a not-eating disorder.

However, just like the health and overweight connection that we have just investigated, it is of no use whatsoever just handing you out another list of 'superior' eating habits. Without a nice big side order of changed belief system, I might as well just tell you to swallow a load of rubbish!

On the other hand, if we ignore what you eat altogether, I am not fulfilling the key objective of the Ideal Weight Programme – which is to hold hands with you until you accelerate away by yourself to your own Ideal Weight. This chapter about food, then, is not a list of recipes. Rather, it is one ingredient of your recipe for life.

The most remarkable experiment

A few years ago a very interesting experiment was conducted in Israel. Do you remember that I told you much earlier that you already knew exactly what you should be eating and that I would prove it to you?

I was one of a group of psychologists given access to the children of a kibbutz. It was a marvellous opportunity to thoroughly test one of the most challenging of all beliefs about food.

The children were all aged between five and nine and the experiment went on for about three weeks, with the full approval of their parents, who fed their children their usual morning and evening meals. The parents did not participate in, or influence, the experiment.

We erected a big tent and set up a long trestle table. The children were allowed unrestricted access to the tent during the day.

On the table we laid out food. At one end was complete junk – sugar products, sweets and snacks. At the other end were lots of fresh salads and fruit. There were all kinds of sauces, breads, cheeses, fats and spreads available.

At lunchtime a full range of hot foods, ranging from junk such as chips through to lightly cooked meats and fish was brought in.

The observers kept a discreet watch on the proceedings. They did not interfere at all.

For the first few days, the kids were in and out of the tent all the time. They went straight for the sweets and all the junk treats. They gorged themselves on the trash with no regard to mealtimes.

After about a week, significant changes began to set in. The empty sugar foods were going out of fashion. Most of the eating was taking place around lunchtime, when hunger would be starting to set in after the gap of several hours since breakfast. White meat and cooked vegetables were being eaten more and more.

By the end of the three weeks, a complete transition had taken place. The children had all gravitated to the healthy end of the table. They turned up at much the same time and ate much the same foods as each other. Fatty meats and heavily cooked vegetables had lost their appeal, as had heavy sauces and just about anything with a lot of sugar or salt in it.

Most popular were dishes such as lightly cooked fish with plenty of salad. Water had become the number one drink instead of fizzy pops.

What caused the transformation? The answer is simple. Most people, deep down and away from outside pressures, know what is good for them. Given that a kibbutz is already considerably removed from the rampant and high-pressured commercialism of most Westernized societies, we could still further distance the children from external pressure by creating their own and separate eating environment.

Nature rapidly took its course and the children ate what was good for them. There is no miracle in that process – eating properly is as natural as breathing air.

The Ideal Weight Programme is not setting new artificial barriers for your eating habits like every diet before has done. It is liberating your eating – and liberating you from your food and diet obsessions.

As we have seen previously, it is in the food, drug and diet industry's interests to perpetuate certain myths about the food we eat. And as we shall cover in this chapter, there is still some element of confusion regarding diet choices. However, in the vast majority of cases, the choice is clear cut if all the commercial, cultural and emotional clutter is cast aside – you know what is good for you.

With a few specific exceptions, most people hunger for more 'expert information' about food because they are genuinely incapable of facing up to the truth within themselves. The Ideal Weight Programme is about choice and change. You are already quite unlike this majority.

Hunger doesn't hurt – it's starvation that kills

The kibbutz children rapidly recognized to eat only when they were hungry and to stop as soon as they were satisfied.

That one sentence is the only eating prescription in the Ideal Weight Programme. As we have seen, it is completely in line with nature, unlike all the other eating habits we have discussed – and the thousands

Hunger Level Worksheet

To help you understand your 'hunger attacks', use this worksheet. Then read on to find out how you can overcome these to achieve your Ideal Weight. Check off your reasons for eating.

1. It's mealtime so it's time to eat.
2. I'm bored and there's not much else to do.
3. It's there so I'd better eat it now.
4. I can make my own decisions, I'll eat when I want to.
5. Well I've been good. I deserve this.
6. It's a pity to waste good food.
7. It's been offered to me and it's rude to refuse.
8. If I don't eat now, I may not have a chance later.
9. I'll just snack on this while watching TV.
10. I'll hate myself later for bingeing, so what?
11. I'll really start dieting tomorrow.
12. This is the last time I'm ever going to eat this.
13. I just can't help myself.
14. No one can see me, so here goes.
15. I usually eat when I'm tense.
16. I eat when I'm sad.
17. I usually eat when I'm happy.
18. After an argument I usually eat myself sick.

After checking off any of the above that may apply to you, write down any specific reasons why you have overeaten or 'binged' in the past.

_____

_____

_____

_____

_____

we have not. That is the sum total of it; eat when you are hungry and stop when you are satisfied.

To avoid any possible sense of deprivation and to acknowledge social realities, we build this eating pattern around three balanced meals a day. When you are satisfied, you stop eating. This will often entail leaving some of your meal on your plate. It is rare that your plate will be spotless – the Ideal Weight Programme is teaching you how to develop and maintain healthy and fulfilling eating habits, it is not training you for a new career as a high-speed dishwasher! This is how many, many people eat.

Food is to be enjoyed – as is the opportunity for conversation around the table. It is normal and natural to pause during a meal. It is normal and natural not to wolf down every last morsel when your tummy is already bulging. As we have already identified, very little eating is actually triggered by hunger, so we have to get back in tune with the concept.

Hunger is a very broad term. It can range from mild peckishness to desperate famine. The mind will seek out the worst-case scenario and look to avoid risk: 'Hunger is bad. Hunger is famine. Avoid hunger at all costs'.

But the Ideal Weight Programme incorporates a useful tool for you to be able to dismantle this debilitating and misleading connection – just as you are acquiring ample tools for every necessary task.

It is important to recognize basic hunger for what it is and not to ignore it. We have looked at the cycle of feast and famine dieting and how it will inexorably push the dieter's weight up, with an eating frenzy inevitably following the period of artificial restriction.

A miniature episode of this sad serial is often played out several times a day in the diary of the depressed dieter. Everyone of us gets hungry, even slim people. A key difference between the hungry slim person and the hungry fat person is that the former satisfied that hunger, while the latter will often fight that hunger in every possible way.

It is one of the great paradoxes of eating behaviour that the overweight person will often try to battle with the one 'genuine' trigger for eating!

So, the overweight person fights with his or her hunger and tries to ignore it. But hunger will always catch up with you in the end. It is as powerful a force as beginning to panic for air when you try to swim under water for longer than you can manage. You crash to the surface, gasping and panting, trying to draw as much air as possible into your desperate lungs.

A similar thing happens to the dieter who tries to ignore hunger for too long. It sets off desperate bingeing. A little healthy snack – or a mealtime brought forward – would have provided perfect satisfaction. The upshot of the misplaced denial is rampant overeating, a ruptured schedule and massive guilt.

For painless and permanent weight loss, the mind and the body need to be in tune with one another, not fighting each other.

When you learn to satisfy your hunger, without overeating, you will, perhaps for the first time since you were a small child, begin to experience normal hunger again – instead of the distorted and extreme hunger that you have habitually created for yourself. Gradually, this 'normal' hunger will become a natural and painless bodily indicator. You don't panic and go into frantic denial mode every time your body suggests that before too long it would like to go to the toilet, do you?

No, of course you don't. You have a choice. You can often hold out for a while and get some more work or play in before you decide that you had better satisfy the urge before things start to become uncomfortable, or you will satisfy the urge immediately because that is more convenient for your schedule.

This is the attitude that the Ideal Weight Programme will develop with you in regard to your hunger levels. We don't preach the benefit of any particular foods to the exclusion of any others but we have found that a couple of pieces of extra fruit a day can be excellent and effective 'gap stoppers'.

However, just recently one of our counsellors from the Ideal Weight Club network told me a story about how it can take a little time and concentration to get back into tune with realistic hunger and eating patterns.

A woman said she was making excellent progress with the course. She said she was taking three modest and balanced meals a day and that her overall anxiety levels with regard to food were considerably down. She was generally pleased with her progress – except she was not losing weight.

The counsellor talked through the possible causes and it transpired that the lady in question was eating up to twenty oranges and twenty pears each day in-between meals!

She was still associating mild and natural hunger pangs with famine, anxiety and deprivation. The best tool to overcome these problems is the following exercise – it worked rapidly for this woman and it will work for you.

The Hunger Scale

Let's check in with your hunger levels. Let's imagine that hunger runs from 0 to 10. If you are ten out of ten, then you are 100 percent stuffed. Maybe you might get like that once a year at Christmas dinner. It is not a state for regular repetition! Remember clearly how overly-full that feels. That is beyond satisfaction. You are fit to burst.

0 out of 10 is starving. It is highly unlikely that you have ever been this hungry, and there is little chance that you ever will be. This is the desperate hunger of a plane crash survivor walking foodless for days in search of rescue.

Remember what we have already stressed about there being no extremes in your new eating regime. Our Hunger Scale allows you to start eliminating these damaging extremes with a solid measurement that you will rapidly learn to calibrate from your own needs.

It will take some working at, but the result will be a precision instrument more valuable than the most expensive watch.

If you are getting down towards one on the scale, you have let yourself get too hungry. Take control and simply have a snack or bring your next mealtime forward.

If you ever feel that you are approaching 9 when

you are eating, simply stop eating because you have had too much already.

Around 6 is the feeling you should be teaching yourself to experience at the end of one of your three main meals – pleasantly satisfied but by no means bloated.

You should learn to come automatically to the meal table at around the 2 to 3 mark. If you are down at this level and it is still quite a while to your next meal – you are just learning your superior control, or maybe you have just done some particularly strenuous work, then don't wait and suffer, only to stuff yourself up to 9 at the next meal. Have a snack but just knock yourself back up to, say the 4 level. If you are right down to 2 but the mealtime is perhaps only an hour-and-a-half away, but you are going to wait for your wife or husband, then just put yourself up to 3.

I want you to put all the visualization powers that we have developed together in making the Hunger Scale work for you. Get in touch with your hunger levels over the next few weeks and start taking mental notes – written notes are preferable for the first fortnight or so – of what is happening to your hunger levels.

Used properly, the Hunger Scale can immediately smash the bingeing cycle. Thereafter it will permanently train you in the art of recognizing and controlling your natural hunger cycle.

You will separate out healthy hunger from destructive panic and you will learn to start feeding your body, not your emotions.

After a few weeks, your use of the Hunger Scale

will be completely automatic. It will have trained you so well in the superior eating patterns of your Ideal Weight Programme that you will no longer even notice that it is there – but you can always reach out and check it is still functioning if you ever feel you need it.

Write down what your hunger level is at the moment. Think of a 0 and then think of a 10 and ask your subconscious where you are at the moment. Do this regularly over the next two weeks.

Get in touch with your hunger levels. It's easy when you know how. The next time you think about needing to go to the toilet, just have a little laugh about how difficult you used to find it to gauge your hunger levels. It should be just as simple a body function.

But the most serious part of the whole Hunger Scale experience, which is one of the key structural supports of the entire Ideal Weight Programme, is that it destroys the obsessive and counterproductive backbone of the conventional diet industry – the degrading and self-defeating practice of endlessly counting calories.

This inane process is of even less relevance to your purpose than it would be to stop your car at every milestone during a long journey when you already know exactly where you have come from and exactly where your destination lies.

Of course calories still count – but they are nothing more or less than units of energy to fuel your body. The point of the Ideal Weight Programme is that calories do count, it is just that you do not have to count them!

111

The ugly side to 'looking good'

Psychologists and historians who have studied human behaviour during warfare have found that battle behaviour is very different to the all-action images of the movie screen. Only a small minority of the soldiers ever try to engage in combat. Only some of them actually fire their weapons and many of them remain cowering behind whatever shelter is available to them.

A lot of the diet industry is like this. Many soldiers won't fight because they have no fundamental belief in the cause. Diets aren't followed either, because those trying to use them don't truly believe that they will work.

More than that, they secretly KNOW that the diet is a load of rubbish and either get involved half-heartedly or toss the manual on to their growing pile of past fads, cons and fantasies. These people are in effect surrendering before they properly begin because they do not believe in the cause.

We have already established that unless a person's belief systems regarding food and eating are substantially changed, it is extremely dubious whether even sound new advice will sway them to improve their habits permanently.

So, with the torrent of nonsense that is constantly churned out, it is hardly surprising that so many confused and anxious 'dieters' shelter ineffectually behind all their books, courses, gadgets and pills, just as the unconvinced soldier cowers behind his sandbags.

A recent survey suggested that while a quarter of all British adults say that they are on a diet at any one time, only 4 percent of them manage to keep their weight down. The number of Americans who say they are trying to lose weight at any given time – 40 million – is fast approaching the equivalent of the entire population of England!

In a study in 1994 by the UK Advertising Standards Authority of thirty-one slimming advertisements, two-thirds were found to have made unreasonable claims.

Some British politicians are now beginning to press for legislation to regulate the industry. It is being suggested that advertisements and schemes that say they can offer rapid weight loss should be subject to government health warnings.

Repackaging bizarre eating habits

Go to the dieting section of any general bookshop. It is liable to be extensive. Now go to the sections on how to develop world peace, how to solve famine and how to end mass unemployment. Hard luck . . . though a diligent assistant may be able to find you the odd book or two. What we read both reflects and frames the values of our society.

I was in a bookshop in New York recently, browsing through the dieting section. I could have been there for days. One book that did catch my eye was *The Ultimate Secret of Losing Weight – Guaranteed to Work!* I just had to see this one.

It was as good as they come – much, much better than most dieting books. On each of its 120 pages it stated in big, bold type 'STOP EATING SO MUCH!'

There are no magic pills, or drinks, or capsules, or whatever that can permanently develop controlled eating habits to make and keep you slim. There are no weird and wonderful diets to replace the simple nutritional instincts that men and women are not allowed to follow for themselves. There is no fantastic diet chewing gum. Neither will prayers nor tears make and keep you slim and, as we have seen, nor will New Year resolutions.

Yes, *The Ultimate Secret or Losing Weight – Guaranteed to Work!* is, in its own way, a very fine book. At least it contains the true key to weight loss, unlike so much other advice.

The only problem, just like all the other systems, is that it fails to tell you how to stop eating so much. It is only a couple of inches from the brain to the mouth. For many people it is the longest journey they ever take – and very many of them, at various stages, simply fall by the wayside.

I don't need to tell you about all the different diets and weight-loss systems that are out there. You have probably tried them. Most of them are very misleading; some of them are very expensive.

And don't be tempted by those large signs and slogans promising 'instant' weight loss. Independent nutritionists agree that rapid weight loss is wrong. The Ideal Weight Programme will usually allow you to lose an average of one pound per week. This is good and this is healthy.

Losing a lot of weight suddenly strips the body of lean tissue as well as fat. That is a nice way of saying that you are cooking up meals of your own muscles and vital organs when you crash diet.

Furthermore, in this crash diet scenario, when the highly artificial and restricted regime is relaxed – the alternative is rapid death through starvation – then much of the weight tends to return, only as fat.

As fat burns fewer calories than lean tissue, the dieter is adding yet another problem. By changing his or her body composition in this way, the person is increasing the future likelihood of excess weight re-occurring and decreasing the body's ability to remove it.

There is one further problem. When food intake is dramatically cut, the body activates its inbuilt survival mechanism which causes the metabolic rate to fall – it basically turns down the boiler to as low as possible. As the restricted regime is relaxed, it takes a while for the metabolic rate to climb back up again, making weight gain inevitable.

Never fall for the misconception, as is perpetuated with high protein diets, that the body does not need carbohydrates. Far from it. A substance known as glycogen is a very important storehouse of energy. When the body is starved of carbohydrates, glycogen is lost along with a lot of body fluids. This regime robs the body of vital energy and water.

Now, round up every single diet book or course you have hoarded (I am now talking about nutrition or recipe material). Find any diet pills, powders or potions (I am not talking about nutritional supplements). Put them all in a bin bag and throw them away. They are crutches you no longer need as you are now putting in some of the final pieces in the jigsaw of your Ideal Weight Programme.

Think of the daftest thing you have ever done with

regard to dieting. Draw up an image of yourself that now seems silly. Imagine yourself – a new slim and totally content you being in the scene. Laugh at the situation and move on from it. That is not you any more.

No recipes but let's get a few things straight

We can't all set up a trestle table under a tent in the Middle East deserts every day to confirm the correctness of our nutritional instincts like those who observed the children on the kibbutz. And while we may now have seen through the lies surrounding the sugar and/or fat-stuffed foods and drinks that have misled and comforted us from childhood, there is always tomorrow's brilliant advertising campaign, and tomorrow's temptations.

To reiterate. Most of us eat too much and a lot of us eat far too much. In particular we eat far too much sugar and fat. It makes us fat and makes us die younger.

I told you this would not be a book with pages of menus. There are some excellent sources to consult for sound food advice, ranging from the fascinating findings of the UK's National Advisory Committee on Nutrition Education back in the early 1980s, through to more recent and comprehensive advice from the World Health Organization. However, this section is partly to dispel a few lingering myths but also to provide a trestle table for everyone.

Portion proportion

Beware! Just like the process of getting fatter itself, portions are getting bigger. When I was a child, we were bought our sugar-poison in little two-ounce open bags. These days sweets come pre-sealed in bags many times that size.

Everything suddenly seems to be in 'family' size portions, which assume a very extended family! If you visit the United States, the burgers in fast food restaurants have become big enough for two people, and the bagels are the size of old-fashioned loaves.

Soft drinks come in 'slammer' sizes, sausages as 'dinner' sausages, biscuits as 'selections' and everything is presented to make bigger appear more economical.

But it means that the poison is coming in bigger doses.

Sugar

Sugar comes in many different forms: sugar itself, icing sugar, caster sugar, muscovado sugar, brown sugar, demerara sugar, molasses, treacle, golden syrup, maple syrup, honey etc. These are all sugars. They vary from having precious little nutritional value besides calories to having absolutely none at all.

There are also some other words for specific types of sugar. They are used in many things but one of the latest tricks of the food industry is to use these words to 'hide' sugar in places you would not expect to find a lot of sugar: 'sports' drinks, baby food and fruit juices. These include glucose, fructose, lactose and maltose.

It is trashy sugar that has done a lot to give all carbohydrates a bad name – sugar is a carbohydrate, and while these can be very useful for the body, sugar is a particularly useless one.

With very few exceptions, all these sugars are empty of vitamins, minerals, fibre, proteins and starch. They displace healthy foodstuffs in our diet. Look at the ingredients of packaged and tinned foods. You will find sugar, under its various guises and disguises in a mind-boggling variety of foods: sausages, beefburgers, vegetables, sauces etc. Sugar is useless. Cut your sugar intake by at least half.

Dairy foods

Good old dairy foods – the idyll of country life and the romance of the butter churn!

Until very recently, butter, milk and cheese were expensive luxuries that relatively few people could afford to eat in anything but tiny amounts. The quantity of milk, butter, cheese and cream that we consume today is far, far greater than in any other century.

We have already seen how milk is automatically thought of as a protein food – it would be better reclassified as a fat food. Taken as a whole, dairy products supply on average between a quarter and a third of our total fat intake and about 40 percent of harmful saturated fat intake.

Vast areas of the world do not consume dairy products. It is a fallacy that dairy products are a completely 'natural' foodstuff.

Spread your butter very thinly. Stop lumping it into vegetables and sauces. Enjoy cheese as a thinly-cut treat rather than in hunks. Grate it and use it sparingly in cooking. Drink semi-skimmed – or preferably skimmed – milk and you can still enjoy all the benefits of milk. The advantages of drinking full-fat milk are far outweighed by the harm that the fat does to our arteries. Switch the adults in your household over to skimmed milk, although check with your doctor what is best for your children, as they have special dietary requirements.

Eggs are a separate case. Here, many experts agree that the total amount per week should be no more than three or four and that includes the 'unseen' eggs used in baking. It might be nice to enjoy one or two eggs at weekend breakfasts and forgo them during the week.

Meat, poultry and fish

Like milk, the benefit of consuming large quantities of meat is vastly outweighed by the proportion of harmful saturated fat it contains. Man has evolved with only limited supplies of meat. The human race has only recently consumed meat in large quantities and that is only for a minority

Cut down on the overall amount of meat you eat and try to cut out entirely processed meats, sausages and pies.

But do still enjoy the meat you eat. You will find that it will cost no more to enjoy a few slices of really tender good meat than it will to load your plate with fatty cuts such as brisket and chops.

Cut off all visible fat and drain and strain off the residue before serving, or before making sauces and gravies.

Eat more poultry, being careful to remove the skin and any fatty sections.

Eat more fish of all kinds – it is very good for you. Include fresh mackerel and herring, which as well as being relatively cheap, contain large quantities of valuable fish oils.

The Ideal Weight Programme is not about deprivation. It may, however, force you to become a more inventive cook, which is a fascinating pastime in itself.

If you simply incorporate the few ideas that have just been outlined, you will dramatically lower your intake of sugar and fat. Enjoying a little fillet steak or spreading a thin layer of butter on a delicious slice of fresh bread is not going to harm you at all. Far from it. Neither is the odd slice of homemade fruitcake. It is the constant gorging and the vast quantities of fat and sugar commonly consumed that do the damage.

There is both the damage to our arteries and the damage to our waistlines. Fat is especially dangerous in both contexts. US researchers experimented by switching eighteen women, all with very low levels of physical activity, from a diet drawing around 37 percent of calories from fat – roughly the American average – to one that was only 20 percent fat. Over twenty weeks, the women lost four to five pounds, even though their overall calorie intake was slightly increased!

It is a fact that calories derived from fat tend to turn to stored bodyfat much more easily than calories derived from other sources.

An obsession with fat appears to be the latest craze, particularly among US diet commentators. A recent issue of the highly respected *Newsweek* magazine featured a highly prominent eight-page investigation of the subject. In that peculiar way of journalism, the article reflected on the obsession and, by dwelling on the subject in such enormous detail, both admitted to sharing the obsession and ended up confirming it!

I mention this because, as in many things dietary, what begins in the United States often ends up elsewhere. Many American dieters have turned their diet obsession on to fat grams. They will buy an extra-low fat pizza and then guzzle the whole lot by themselves! They will feel virtuous for having selected the zero-fat cookies from the bewildering array on display – and then go home and scoff the lot while watching TV.

Avoid the obsession with all single issues. The Ideal Weight Programme is about moderation in all things – it is just that we have to be especially modest about fat and sugar!

Some of the other things you should consider include:

- Eat plenty of bread. Eat bread with at least two of your three meals per day. If there is any such thing as a 'traditional', then it is bread. Enjoy a variety of bread, but try to avoid the most processed of white breads – a lot of nutritional value has been removed. Try to incorporate more wholemeal bread into your diet – ask for it specifically because it is exceptionally good for you. Spread your bread sparingly and get used to enjoying it, as well, just used to soak up the juices (not fat!) from your meals. These simple recommendations for bread would vastly improve the average diet without leaving anyone feeling deprived. Also get used to a slice of bread as a snack instead of something sugar based.

- Eat fresh food in preference to things that come in packets, boxes, cartons, bottles, tubes and bags. It is much less likely that the food has been seriously tampered with, such as being bulked out with useless or even harmful substances. Unlike money, a lot of food does actually grow on trees (or on bushes, or in fields). Get back in touch with this fact. It will save your heart, your waistline and, often, it will also save money. Remember, there is no 'convenience' in processed foods.

- Eat plenty of fresh fruit and vegetables. Do not overcook your vegetables – just wash them and cook them lightly – but get used to piling them up on your plate where the chips and fatty meat used to be. Vegetables do not make you fat – it is the butter and fatty and sugary sauces that do that. Mash up lovely fluffy potatoes with skimmed milk.

- Thicken sauces by reducing them or using flour, or

arrowroot, or breadcrumbs, instead of butter and cream. Use water or skimmed milk as a base.

- Get rid of the salt cellar from the table and stop adding extra salt to meals. Excess salt is a major factor in heart disease and high blood pressure. There is ample salt in the unprocessed foods we already eat, and salt is classically abused, as in crisps and fried nuts, to encourage you to eat more.

- Do go into a good natural food store and start to educate yourself about the fantastic range of cheap spices and herbs available. Not only will your meals be tasting better because everything is fresh but you can add superb extra flavour at a tiny cost.

- Cut down drastically on the amount of frying you do. The microwave, the grill, a steamer and the oven should be the chief areas of food preparation. But do not be too obsessed with cooking – sometimes raw, particularly with many salads, can be nicest.

- As well as vegetables, get used to plenty of rice and pasta with your main meals. Both can be mixed with delightful dressings and chopped fruit and vegetables. Both methods taste much better than smothering the rice or pasta in sweetened fats.

- When you do fry, or when you need a little oil for a dressing, pick olive oil. Choose the best you can afford. It has become much more easily available and more keenly priced in the supermarkets in recent years and, as you will only be using a little, choose a really good one. As well as olive oil, have a look at all the interesting vinegars that have become available. Mixed with chopped herbs they can make wonderful dressings for your food.

- Be moderate in your alcohol intake. We have already dealt with many of the urges that drive people to excessive drinking – they are the same as for eating. But, if you enjoy drink, then enjoy it even more. With the money you save from cutting down, treat yourself to a superb bottle of wine – the difference between a good bottle of wine and an outstanding one may often be only the price of a few glasses of cheap lager.

That last point about the excellent wine is central to the philosophy of the Ideal Weight Programme. As we have stressed, it is not about deprivation. It is about three normal balanced meals a day, and the odd snack if you need one. It is about quality as well. You will enjoy your food much more, not only because of the wonderful changes that are happening to your body and to your life but also because your food is much tastier and more satisfying. It is quite possible that your range of flavours to date has been dominated by sugar, salt and monosodium glutamate. That is a very poor representation of what nature has cheaply and readily on offer.

From wine as a treat to water as a way of life

Most people drink far too little water and far too much tea, coffee and alcohol, as well as sugar-laden rubbish. Drink more water instead and the calories, the drugs and the poisons of these other liquids are dramatically reduced.

Drinking more water brings a host of other health benefits: fluid retention is reduced (the body is hanging on to fluid because it is being fed too little); muscle and skin tone can be improved. Many people suffer from constipation and water relieves this distressing condition; further, bingeing and over-eating urges are reduced as simple thirst no longer becomes bound up with hunger and eating.

Replace most of your other drinks with water and aim to take about eight medium-sized glasses of water a day. The benefits will rapidly show as the process of looking and feeling better accelerates for you.

Remember, however, that while it is good for you, water doesn't have any 'magic' properties! It won't make you lose weight by itself, or wash or 'melt' away fat, as some people believe. But it is important as part of a healthy daily routine.

There were no lists of orders in this chapter, just some recommendations. Hopefully a few lingering myths have been unscrambled and you have learnt how to lay out a very appetizing trestle table for yourself, your friends and your family!

7

Making new habits stick

Let's go back for a few moments to the new film script we have been putting together – you starring and directing in the movie of your Ideal Weight Programme. As the finished picture fast approaches, ending with a happy you, slim for life, it is time we did a quick screen-test to prove to you just how advanced your cinematic talents have become.

Swish away the old you

A little while ago we went through the benefits of fresh food. Find an example for yourself of something you have usually bought packaged that you will always buy fresh in future ... carrots or bread or meat? See the old you taking it off the supermarket shelf and putting it into your basket. This is the old you and you are overweight.

Hold that picture on screen one. Take a second

screen. This is the new you and you are slim. You have walked past the packaged items and are getting the equivalent but superior product from the fresh vegetable section, the fresh bread section, or the fresh meat counter, or whatever. What is more, you are slim.

Go back to the first picture. See yourself, see the packaged food, see the overweight.

Now put a small box of the second picture into the bottom corner of the first screen – just like you sometimes see on TV sports or news reports. See the new slim you. See the fresh food.

Now, look at the whole screen, with the second screen down in the corner. Look at everything. See the old and new pictures and then – the second picture swishes up from the bottom and covers the whole screen. Swish! – and that is the new you. It feels great.

Put all that together and do it a few times right now. Really enjoy the feelings it creates for you.

It's not a problem if you can handle it

Just as bad eating habits are not inborn, so worrying is learned. Children imitate what they observe in their parents. Our parents taught us to worry and we have been teaching this to our own children. Worrying does not solve problems and it brings nothing but harmful stress reactions. It is the way that you create your own stress.

Worrying is a destructive habit which causes stress in your body. Every time a worry-thought goes through your mind, a corresponding tension is experienced physically. If you sit and worry about money, you may well begin to feel a tightness in your tummy. This could be the start of ulcers or colitis. If you sit around and worry about being fat, the nagging ache in your stomach could be picked up as hunger pangs and may trigger unnecessary eating.

Worry and fear are addictive emotions. Worry and fear are habits much like smoking and over-eating. Worry and fear create their own rush, a high if you like, as would be gained from drug-taking.

However unpleasant this may seem, these habit patterns of worry and fear are addictive. They have their own symptoms, such as anxiousness, sleeplessness, butterflies in the stomach, sweaty palms and increased blood pressure. They are negative, harmful and can lead to overweight. We must break them – and we can, surprisingly easily.

But let me first outline specific mind-types that I have found over the years are frequently associated with weight problems.

There is the overall victim syndrome. There are two ways of seeing the world in terms of who is in control of your life. Either you are in control or 'they' are in control. If you are in control, then the chances are that you see life as a challenge. By coming this far with the Ideal Weight Programme you have shown that you can face challenge. If you feel helpless in your life, then you have adopted the 'victim' psychology. You feel that 'they' are running your life for you.

One manifestation of this syndrome is the 'poor me' attitude: 'poor me, look how hard I try and no matter what happens, no one ever appreciates me'.

This is a game played by you in which you will never be the winner.

Then there is the 'blame game'. Helplessness is developed and reinforced by the attitude of 'if it weren't for the bus, the weather, the economy, the customers etc., I could have . . .'

There is also the martyr, or rescuer, mentality. The martyr assumes responsibility for everyone else's problems but in the process loses responsibility for him or herself. The martyr confuses love with pity and labours under a false belief system that holds that it is good to suffer.

Suppressing emotions can also amplify stress within the body and is often associated with deviant eating patterns and overweight. Many physical illnesses are influenced by such suppression and these include asthma, colitis, ulcers, persistent headaches, insomnia, bronchitis and high blood pressure. A very common symptom of suppressed emotions is shallow and laboured breathing.

A relaxed body cannot contain a destructive thought – proper relaxation breaks all these destructive cycles, all of which can trigger anxiety and eating.

Your abilities to relax have been mounting steadily throughout this book. The Affirmations you have for ever. Simply copy them out and recall all the positive associations that have already developed. You can also take the situation that is causing pain, catch it and squash it and make the letter O. A very simple accompaniment to this is to close your eyes and take in several long and deep breaths, blowing the air out as if your are blowing out a candle.

Another method, now you have become proficient with visualization techniques, is to put yourself into that situation and see yourself taking it in your stride. Do that several times until you feel the confidence and competence oozing into the situation.

So, you see that you already have a considerable array of tools at your disposal to dispel the kind of emotional build-ups that can undermine your Ideal Weight Programme. We are saving the best tool until last and before long you shall own that one too.

Passing it on – the Ideal Weight Programme and children

'If only I had known about this programme when I was young, then I would never have been fat.' Lots of people who come to the clinic or the clubs say that.

Well, it wasn't around – certainly not all pulled together and published like this – when you were young, but we can do the next best thing: we can stop the next generation suffering from the influences that created all our habit patterns.

Everyone establishes role models. Far and away the most important initial role models in any child's life are its parents. If there is one overweight parent, the child has an approximately 50 percent risk of also becoming overweight. The risk rises significantly if both parents are overweight.

There is a horrible and harmful syndrome where some parents have forced their children to endure some of the bizarre and unhealthy dieting practices that they themselves, in their desperation and confusion, have tried.

The key difference to appreciate with the Ideal Weight Programme is that its dietary recommendations are totally in line with the healthiest and most realistic practices that science has yet recommended. The programme is about healthy and enjoyable feeding of the body – not putting strange and unnatural demands on it.

Children are not, except in very rare cases of medical abnormality, born fat. They are programmed to be fat. They become the class bully or the class clown at school in order to compensate. Whatever the outcome, it is likely that they will suffer in some way for being different.

It is vital that a child is never allowed to feel deprived or neglected. From the earliest ages food must not be associated with anything other than what it really is – fuel for our bodies.

All learning processes for young children should be fun. Learning about animals and nature and their brothers and sisters is fun. Learning to read and write is fun. Make sure that learning about food is fun, too – it is as easy as making any of the above subjects fun. Tell your children interesting facts about food at mealtimes. Involve them in the preparation of food and talk to them about it.

Do not surround your children with rules regarding food. The Ideal Weight Programme does not surround adults with rules regarding food – they would simply rebel.

Children will rebel, too. Lecturers will be ignored.

Simply do not build your relationship with your children around food. Discipline is not dependent on food, nor is motivation, learning, reward, comfort, or love.

Hugs, books, toys, outings, kisses, special trips, bike rides, holidays and a simple holding of hands are just a few of endless behavioural associations that do not rely on food. Would you give a two-year-old a tranquillizer every time he or she is upset. No, of course not. Then why give them food.

There should be no banned foods. Remember, children burn calories at a much faster rate than you or I. The odd bit of chocolate will not harm them and is no big deal. The only big food deals for children are the ones that their parents create for them. It does not matter, though, if your children are already growing up. You may feel that you have lost out but it is far, far from the case.

Everything about the Ideal Weight Programme is a gain. Do not pressurize your children or seek confrontation with them in any way. Do not try to force your new belief structures on to them. Just accept that gradual change will come. Introduce treats from outside the world of calories. Concentrate on the benefits of your new lifestyle. Changes for the whole family will come if you quietly lead by example. If you push and pull, the only guaranteed outcome is tension.

Fill your children with love and fill them with healthy and nutritious food. Do not fill them with hang-ups about food. Break the cycle that is passed on from parent to child. Your objective should be to make the Ideal Weight Programme redundant within a single generation.

Fit for your life

This is an appropriate time so discuss the simple activity programme that we have several times affirmed that we shall incorporate into our lives.

As in the section that has just passed, on stress and relaxation, you will see that the Ideal Weight Programme is covering all angles.

All through my career as a psychologist I have had a deep distrust of drugs. They do not solve problems – they merely contain them within people's minds and leave them there to fester and re-occur.

There is one single exception. These are the natural drugs – the hormones – that your body creates. When physical activity is undertaken, the body releases its own natural relaxation hormones. Breathing is also increased, so – as we have just seen in relation to stress relaxation and deep breathing – you are immediately provided with a secondary relaxant.

You will notice that I am not using the word 'exercise' and this is for particular reasons. You may have tried a lot of exercise programmes in the past as a primary component of weight loss programmes. The Ideal Weight Programme believes that this is a radically flawed approach. Strenuous sport is great for those who enjoy playing it – just as quantum physics can be great fun for those who understand and study it.

Strenuous exercise is a poor component of a weight loss programme. It is dangerous and it takes a huge amount of exercise to lose the calories that it would be far easier not to put into your mouth in the first place.

The Ideal Weight Programme carefully uses its activity schedule for specific purposes. The first is for the crucial relaxation effect that we have already discussed.

The second is related to calories. Before widespread car ownership and the onset of more sedentary lifestyles, it is estimated that the average person's daily calorific requirement was at least 500 higher. The incorporation of an activity programme gives more leeway in your dietary requirements. It takes away the strictness and allows for a few more ups and downs.

The third, and critically important element, is to fine-tune your metabolism. Years of over-eating, under-eating and whatever have left vast numbers of lifelong dieters with disrupted metabolisms, with a slow metabolic rate constantly exacerbating any tendency towards overweight. The rate will not increase hugely but, over the course of the months and years ahead, it will make a huge difference.

The fourth reason is a similar issue. You will remember that yo-yo dieting, particularly over a long period, will change the body's composition. While overall average weight may remain largely unchanged, the proportion of fat to lean tissue will increase. Many people who are only a little overweight may be considerably overfat. We have already discussed how fat cells burn fewer calories than lean tissue cells. Being overfat can help to trap you in a vicious cycle of remaining fat.

The fifth reason is one of health and underlines the Ideal Weight Programme's philosophy. You are painlessly and permanently seeking to become slim for reasons – not to conform with fads, fashions, or other people's agenda. Various long-term studies in the US have revealed interesting connections between activity, overweight and health.

One study divided 119 overweight men and 112 overweight women into three separate groups; a calorie-controlled and low-fat diet regime; the same diet plus three moderate aerobic activity sessions per week; no diet adjustment and no activity. After a year, the diet-only group had lost significant levels of fat compared with the unaltered group.But the diet-plus-activity group not only lost even more fat but they also significantly reduced their risk of heart disease.

In another study of 13,000 middle aged men and women, it was discovered that, overall, the fittest men had a death rate less than one-third of that of the least fit. For women there was a more than fourfold difference. The rates for cardiovascular disease were even more dramatically affected by fitness.

It is also a fact that many of the unpleasant conditions and diseases that fatness helps to create, fitness can help to diminish. Like everything in the Ideal Weight Programme, the jigsaw is fitting together with a satisfying snap!

The sixth reason is simple. Activity tones you up. You are already losing the weight, you might as well look great!

Getting Going

We are going to go to our trestle table again. But this time the issue is not to prove that you know what to eat; the question is, how fit are you and what do you need to do? I'm not going to tell you!

The Ideal Weight Programme does recommend that all participants take a medical check-up with their doctor before they participate. It is not that we are advocating anything restrictive or an unhealthy diet or any unduly taxing exercise. It is simply good practice and good reassurance.

There is one magic activity that is the bedrock of the programme and it is absolutely free. Walking. We recommend that you do it twice a day.

Habitual couch potatoes do not need to seek out anything more strenuous than walking and it is something that everyone should do on a regular basis. Research has shown that the chief benefits of all exercising come when people move from a sedentary lifestyle to moderate activity – the daily equivalent of thirty minutes to one hour of walking.

The chief benefits of walking are improved muscle tone, accelerated weight loss, improved cardiovascular and respiratory fitness and a slowing of osteoporosis, the bone loss that occurs with ageing, particularly in women.

Walking a brisk 15-minute mile burns about as many calories as running the same mile in about half the time, with a hugely reduced risk of injury to areas such as the foot, shin, knee, hip and back.

Get walking twice a day. Cycling is just as good. Do no more than you can very comfortably manage. If that is just a couple of hundred yards to the shops and back instead of driving, then that is absolutely fine. Build up gradually until you are enjoying at least ten minutes of relatively brisk walking twice a day.

The changes you will notice in your body are fantastic.

There are absolutely no rules with activity, just so long as you are underpinning the Ideal Weight Programme with the minimum of two enjoyable brisk walks each day, taking as long as you like to build up.

If you are already super-fit and take loads of exercise but are still overweight, then going into full-time physical training is obviously not the answer – you must still be eating far too much.

If your work already involves a large amount of physical activity, you may like to supplement your regime with a few minutes each day of relaxing yoga exercises, coupled, perhaps, with an occasional few callisthenic exercises such as press-ups.

In fact, work up gradually but remember that the activity is to help your life. Your life is not a slave to exercise. There is a growing trend of 'exercise junkies' – people who fill a void in their lives with obsessive exercise. It is as much an addiction as any other addiction.

Like your eating habits, the activity programme of the overall Ideal Weight Programme is about getting in touch with your real needs, not anyone else's. If your first steps are literally just a few steps, then that is absolutely fine.

You set the pace, not some figure gyrating on your TV screen in multi-coloured lycra. These people can be as de-motivating and downright damaging as all the purveyors of the codswallop diets.

Another fad, again emanating from the US, is the cult of the Fitnevangelists. These people are usually ex-fatties who have spotted that they can make a lot of money by parading their new-found slimness on exercise videos. Believe me, it was a lot more than a little wobbling around that moved vast quantities of weight off them.

Beware. Just as you ultimately choose and maintain your own new eating habits, so it is with your activity programme. Go to it. Being fitter is fun!

8

Using your tape – it's my turn now!

Three balanced meals a day, the odd, snack, some enjoyable physical activity and a powerful new system to keep and to use. Losing about one pound a week on average without even thinking about it and becoming slim painlessly and permanently. I hope you think the Ideal Weight Programme has been worth the effort of getting to know.

There is one other thing. I did promise that the most powerful tool of all was being saved for last. Well, here it is. It's the tape. You've done all the hard work to date. It's my turn now. Sit back and enjoy!

Using the Lose Weight Think Slim tape

Do not listen to this tape while driving, using machinery or in any other situation which demands your full attention.

1. On each side of the tape is a complete programme, making two programmes in total.

2. Listen to programme one, on side one, once a day for two weeks. You may listen to it more often if you wish but once a day is sufficient.

3. After the initial two weeks, listen to programme two, on side two. Once a day for two weeks as before.

4. Establish a comfortable place where you will not be disturbed while listening to your tape.

5. Try to listen to your tape at approximately the same time each day to establish a habit pattern.

6. If you fall asleep when listening to your tape, this is of no consequence. In fact, it has been found that your subconscious mind will absorb the information all the better if you are asleep. The information goes deep into your subconscious mind to be stored and made available whenever it is required.

7. Reference is made within the programmes to our technique of Making the Letter 'O'. This powerful relaxation technique is described in detail on page 61 of this book.

8. Don't feel under pressure: it's not the end of the world if you have to miss a day. If you miss out on one step, simply go back and do it again.
   Good luck!

Lose Weight Think Slim tape progress chart

You may find this a helpful exercise to increase the effectiveness of my tape. It will give you a good idea of your progress as you move towards your Ideal Weight.

Rate yourself from 1 – 10 before and after you listen to your audio tape.

1. Totally relaxed no tension whatsoever
2. Very relaxed
3. Moderately relaxed
4. Fairly relaxed
5. Slightly relaxed
6. Slightly tense
7. Fairly tense
8. Moderately tense
9. Very tense
10. Extremely tense (at breaking point!)

Week of	Before session	After session	Comments
Monday			
Tuesday			
Wednesday			
Thursday			
Friday			
Saturday			
Sunday			

Photocopy or make your own charts similar to above and fill them in on a daily basis in order to ascertain your progress.

9

The secret of my technique

Do you remember that I told you that my lifelong special interest in psychology has been operant conditioning – better known as understanding brainwashing? And do you recall that I have explained that techniques which can enslave can also empower and that we have stressed throughout this book that the choice always remains yours?

Well, you now know a great deal about operant conditioning. You have become extremely good at understanding some of its techniques. What I have been doing is teaching you how to deprogramme yourself, to wash away all the debris that has avalanched down on your eating habits throughout your life.

It is you who have been doing all the exercises in visualization, exercising your mind and building up strength just as you can with any other part of the body.

It is you who have rooted out the reasons and the

anxieties that have not in the past allowed you to painlessly and permanently lose weight.

The cornerstone of the Ideal Weight programme is to put a slim person's belief system into a fat person's body. The entire process of this book is geared towards making you a slim person.

You are now a slim person in the reality of your subconscious mind – your body will catch up soon. That is inevitable. It has already happened to thousands of others. You now think like a slim person. As you think, so you will feel and as you feel, so you will become. It may feel a little strange for the moment but these changes are very real.

The easiest processes for anyone to believe in are processes that they can fully understand, so let me try to explain my process a little further.

The vast majority of habit patterns are developed through repetition – tying your shoelaces, learning to drive etc. – but it has long been a concern of psychology to learn how to change habit patterns quickly.

I have always had a deep distrust of the traditional methods of psychology that look for the precise reasons behind behaviour. Someone may have a fear of spiders. A great deal of time may be expended to find out that when she was two years old, the light in the little girl's bedroom cast a gigantic shadow of a spider on the wall and, as she had earlier seen part of a monster film on television where people were eaten by giant insects, she has been terrified of spiders ever since.

All that is fine – but finding out the reason will not give the girl, who now happens to be, say, 40, any effective strategy to cope with that fear.

The subconscious mind has its own reality. Whether events follow the logic of pure reason is irrelevant. Whether the subconscious mind has been led, or misled, is of no importance. Even after finding out the reasons for the shadow on the wall, the woman would still be terrified the next time she saw a spider.

What has this got to do with painlessly and permanently losing weight? Absolutely everything because if your subconscious mind was still to associate guzzling chocolate with missing love or comfort, then all the encouragement and diet books in the world could not break that association. Psychology – and success in life – is not about endlessly dwelling on the causes of problems, it is about rapidly developing successful strategies to overcome the problem.

You have been inside your own subconscious many times by now and established a slim person's belief system. You have the technique to make whatever changes you may in future wish to make. At will you have become capable of placing powerful new resources and capabilities within your old experience.

The power of your mind

People often refer to me as a hypnotist. I can hypnotize people and I have done so but that is not the key to these extremely powerful techniques. Hypnotism is simply a state of concentrated relaxation that allows access to the subconscious mind. On its own it does nothing; hypnosis is just a tool.

I have seen so called hypnotic solutions to overweight but there can be no guaranteed permanence in the results. 'Don't do' suggestions under hypnosis are often just a screen across the subconscious. Many times the person's beliefs are unchanged and the screen can be knocked over.

Let me give you an example of what is possible within the techniques of the Ideal Weight Programme. When I was at university in America, a young female friend asked me about the area I was involved in and how the system worked.

I knew her steady boyfriend well too and I suggested a quick example with which she could have a little fun. I told her to very gently pull the lobe of his right ear every time he climaxed when they made love for the next few weeks.

About a month later we were all sitting down at a conference. I asked another women I knew to do something for me. I asked her to walk up behind the young man and to very gently pull the lobe of his right ear. This she did. The result was instant, totally predictable and very powerful . . . that is how strong these techniques are.

Let me give you two more examples from my own experience which led me to keep refining my work. I used to be a keen scuba diver. I always had a problem, when deep down underwater, of convincing myself that my air supply was totally 100 percent. My instructor, who was also a good friend, knew my problem and my anxiety – just as I know the problems and anxieties of overweight.

Always, as we were getting down towards the bottom of the dive, he would swim up to me, give my tanks and gear a quick but expert inspection, and then give me a thumbs-up signal.

Whenever he and I passed in the street in future years, he would always give me a thumbs-up. I would immediately feel the air go straight and deep into my lungs and I would experience a delightful surge of confidence.

Another occasion was when I first learnt to fly small aircraft, another favourite hobby. We always used to go out from Dublin airport and, even though I could always take-off and fly OK, my landings were terrible.

One Sunday, I must have bump, bump, bumped down the runway a dozen times before my instructor said: 'Take her back up, Paul, we are going for a fly out around the west'.

A little while later we came across a military airport and radioed in to see if we could land. There was no reply (Ireland tends to be a bit like that on Sundays). I came in to try a landing anyway. It was perfect. We flew back to Dublin and I came in to land. It was perfect.

The habit pattern was smashed because there had been a change in the sequence that had allowed me to succeed. The failure pattern had been broken because I was no longer trying to land in the same place. It was a different me in a different picture – just like you directing and starring in the movie of your Ideal Weight Programme!

And this movie is just like all the other exciting new pictures that you have been in by now. They are totally real to your subconscious and you have been there and felt the different and positive emotions associated with the new and positive behaviour. This is a remarkably powerful system for change.

Let me give a prompt from your own childhood. Can you remember a hymn, a song or a nursery rhyme that you used to sing in school. Can you hear it and see the accompanying scene. Find any scene from your childhood and feel the emotions that rise up.

Your mind is full of keys that set off emotions. Some people's chests puff out when they sing. Then, when they hear their national anthem, their chests puff out automatically because they are subconsciously singing along.

It is important that you understand the basis of these techniques, not that you have to learn all the psychological jargon that sometimes surrounds them. What we are doing is teaching you to talk to your subconscious mind in a language that it understands, believes and will respond to. This is why shouting and screaming and tensed-up attempts to concentrate are doomed to failure. You do not like being shouted and screamed at and neither does your subconscious.

I have a saying that I often repeat in this context. 'a push meets with a push and a pull meets with a pull'. Have you ever seen a 'wet paint' sign and had an urge to touch it? If you are walking down the street and someone says 'don't look round but . . . ', do you not have the urge to look round? Someone recently established that if people in public telephone call boxes see someone waiting, they will automatically stay on the call longer .. . a push meets with a push.

This is why all diet programmes that merely give you lists of orders to follow are also doomed to failure

– they are not in any way teaching you to communicate with your belief systems to change your habit patterns permanently.

Your mind is full by now of positive keys surrounding your new habits. You are automatically programmed as to which end of the trestle table you will head for.

There is nothing hit or miss about the Ideal Weight Programme. Every technique within it has been used to free the enslaved mental prisoners of some of the most evil men of this century. You have been taught how to use these methods for yourself – to free yourself, painlessly and permanently, from a lifetime of fatness and from all the influences that would keep you trapped therein.

10

Top ten tips for achieving your Ideal Weight

1. Plan what food it will be necessary to have in the house before you go shopping. Random shopping leads to random eating.

2. Do not go shopping on an empty stomach. Retailers are experts at putting temptations your way.

3. Unless you live way out in the country, drop the habit of always driving to the shops. Walk there – and think of all the money you are saving every time you do not turn the car on.

4. Eat all snacks sitting down at the same table where you eat all of your main meals. This will make you assess whether you are feeding your body or your emotions.

5. There are a million reasons for keeping junk food in the house. There is one very simple reason not to – it makes and keeps you fat. Banish trashy food and drinks from your house and you banish them from your life.

6. Eating is not a race. Get used to putting down your cutlery between mouthfuls. Chew your food up and enjoy the flavour.

7. Do not let the bad day blues get to you. If it is raining or snowing, then do something you have been delaying within the house. Clean out the attic or the oven, or fix the loose tiles in the bathroom.

8. Establish a treat pattern during your weight loss period. Remember that losing weight is saving you money – how about five pounds a week into a kitty for new clothes?

9. Develop interests in new areas of cookery and gardening – baking your own bread is very satisfying, as is growing herbs and spices (this can be done in window boxes as well).

10. Most of all, don't listen to the dream stealers. Many people will have their own agenda for making comments such as: 'I don't know why you are bothering.' This is their problem, not yours!

11

Some questions and answers

Q. *I am quite overweight; what weight should I aspire to be? I've seen pictures in magazines and read in books that there is a formula to work out how much you should weigh. For example, I read that a woman who is five feet eight inches tall should weigh ten stone. That's about how tall I am: is ten stone my Ideal Weight?*

A. Formulas can be useful from a health point of view, and you should ask your doctor about this. But your Ideal Weight is essentially the weight that you would like to be for the rest of your life. Decide the weight, the shape and the size at which you would feel your best. Perhaps it was the shape and size you were when you left school, got married, or some other time you were really proud of yourself. Your body knows your Ideal Weight. So listen to your body.

Q. *Won't exercise make me thinner? I've seen so many of* *those exercise videos. The people on those programmes all look great . . . Why not me?*

A. Exercise alone will not appreciably help you to lose weight. Research has shown that if, for example, you did three-quarters of an hour of aerobics a day, three days a week, at the end of the year you might have lost eight or nine pounds. That hardly seems worthwhile as a way simply to lose weight. But exercise is very important because it keeps you fit, and I would suggest that you undertake a regular exercise programme. Join a leisure centre. Play golf or tennis, ride a bike, go swimming, do yoga. Get involved with other people – set up a programme, even.

In doing all this, you will become aware of your body, because by becoming aware, you will stimulate your mind and develop the mind control I have been telling you about. You will find that very soon you will become proud of yourself and enjoy the control that you are experiencing. So while exercise alone may not help you lose a lot of weight, it will help keep you on track in the Ideal Weight Programme.

Q. *I've heard that laxatives can help one lose weight, but you don't mention them as part of the Ideal Weight Programme. Can I use them?*

A. Do not take laxatives as a means of losing weight. I cannot stress the danger that may be attached to such a procedure. As you change your eating patterns, however, you may find that you become a little constipated as your bowel adjusts. This should not last long. Natural roughage in the food you eat is the best way to overcome this, but if necessary, you could consider taking a very mild laxative which contains natural ingredients, like Senokot. Do not take any laxatives that contain sugar. And do not take them in order to lose weight.

Q. *I have a very demanding day job, and a lot of responsibilities at home too. I've heard that stress like this affects your weight. Is that true?*

A. Well, when we are under strain our body puts out adrenalin to help us go that extra mile. This adrenalin raises the sugar level in your blood, and this triggers off a release of insulin to balance this. Your blood sugar level will probably end up lower than before. At this point you may feel the need to eat and drink for energy or comfort or to calm your fears, anger or tension. You will probably binge on foods that cannot be converted into useful energy at the time, and put on some extra pounds instead.

To overcome your craving, just go back and listen to side one of your audio tape. The anxiety and tension will soon pass.

Q. *Is there anything I should do before starting the programme?*

A. As with any weight loss programme, you should first have a medical check-up to determine your general state of health.

Second, stop taking over-the-counter diet pills, as these will interfere with the programme's effectiveness.

Third, ensure that you maintain an adequate vitamin intake – in general, one multivitamin tablet a day should suffice, but check with your doctor.

Q. *What about diet pills? Can they help me to lose weight?*

A. There are many pills on the market which claim to help you lose weight. I do not advise you to use them unless recommended to do so by your doctor.

Diet pills will not help you as you follow the Ideal Weight Programme, and you should stop taking them at least two weeks before you start using this book and tape (although check first with your doctor if they are something he or she has specially prescribed for you). In my experience, diet pills and other forms of appetite suppressants will not help you to lose weight permanently. Rather, they tend to have that rebound effect: when people stop taking them, they gain even more weight than they lost while they were on them.

Q. *What about smoking?*

A. Well, that's something your doctor certainly isn't going to recommend! While the nicotine in cigarettes does act as an appetite suppressant (it affects the stomach's secretions), the many harmful effects of smoking far outweigh this dubious benefit of interfering with your body's natural processes. Smoking is no way to control your weight!

If you are stopping smoking, you may find that you put on some weight as you seek to replace that bad smoking habit with a bad eating habit. But by following the Ideal Weight Programme you will learn to control these feelings, so neither smoking nor eating will be an issue.

Q. *At what point should I see my doctor about my weight problem?*

A. It is always a good idea to visit your doctor if you are concerned about a serious weight problem, especially if you seem not to lose weight however hard you try. There is always the possibility that something else may be wrong, of which your excess weight may be a symptom.

Q. *I am losing weight on the Ideal Weight Programme – but only very slowly. Does this mean that something is wrong?*

A. Just as not everyone can run 100 metres in the same time, so it takes us all a slightly different time to achieve our Ideal Weight. But just as if you were running – or even walking! – stick at it and you'll get there.

Q. *Today I went crazy and binged on my favourite foods. I feel terribly guilty. Is this the end of my good intentions?*

A. Of course not! If you have been responding to the Programme up to now and really felt you needed that piece of cake, well, have a couple of day's rest and start again. This happens to everyone!

Q. *I find listening to your tape quite boring and a waste of time. In fact, if I listen to it in bed, I sometimes fall asleep. Can it really work?*

A. However bored or fed up you are, I do still urge you listen to the tape as instructed, over and over again. That way, the information will go deep into your subconscious mind, and become a part of your belief system.

It doesn't matter if you fall asleep while listening to the tape. You needn't fall asleep, but if you do, so much the better! The information will go into your subconscious mind and stay there like a time capsule, ready for instant recall.

A last word

We would be delighted to hear from you as to how you are getting on so that we can share in your success and so encourage others.

We are also always delighted to hear from anyone who wishes to make suggestions on how the Ideal Weight Programme can be more effective, so that we can share these tips with others. We would also welcome your comments on how the Programme has worked for you. So do write to me!

Paul Goldin
Knapton Court
York Road
Dun Laoghaire
Co. Dublin, Ireland